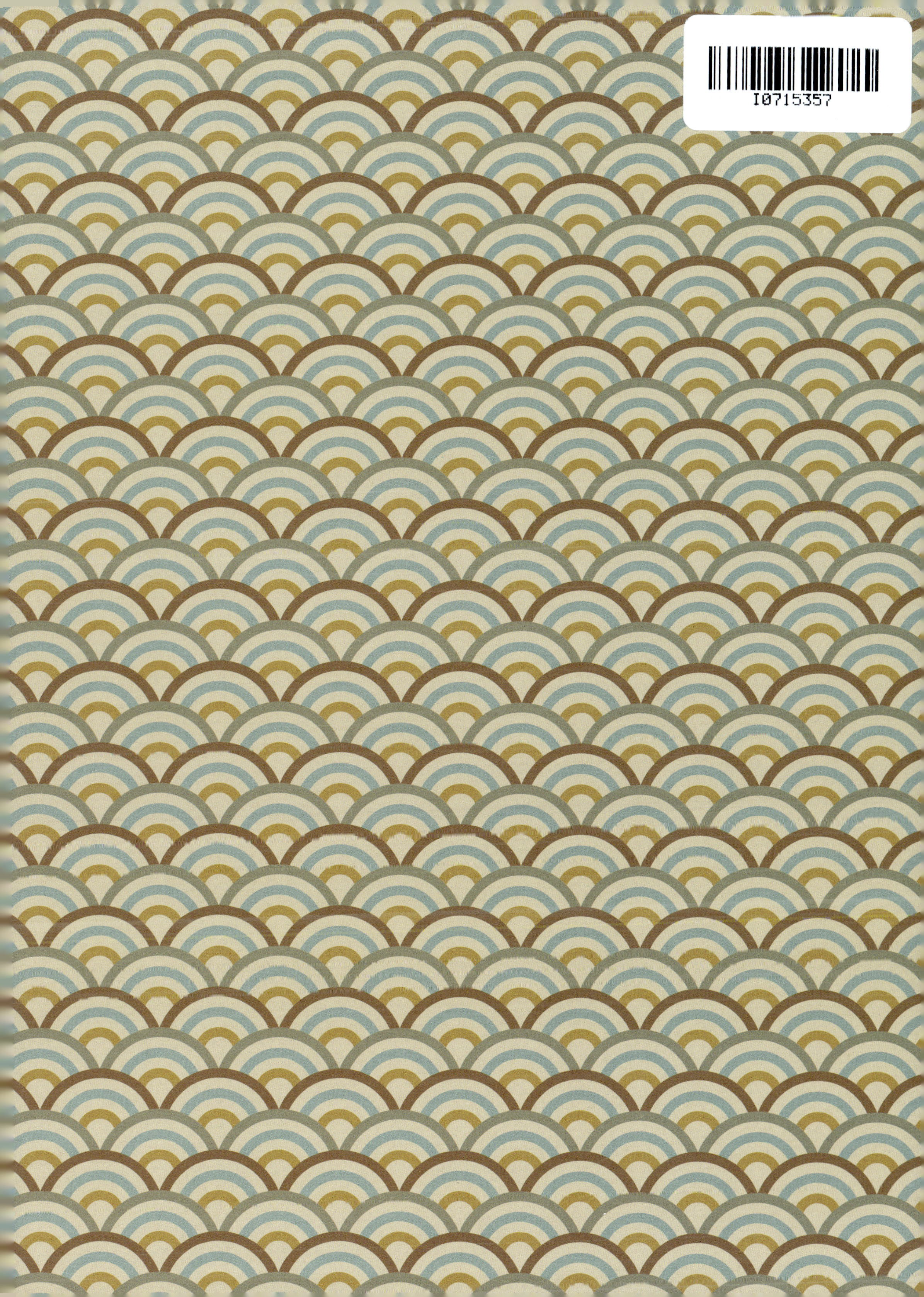
I0715357

ETHEL WALLACE

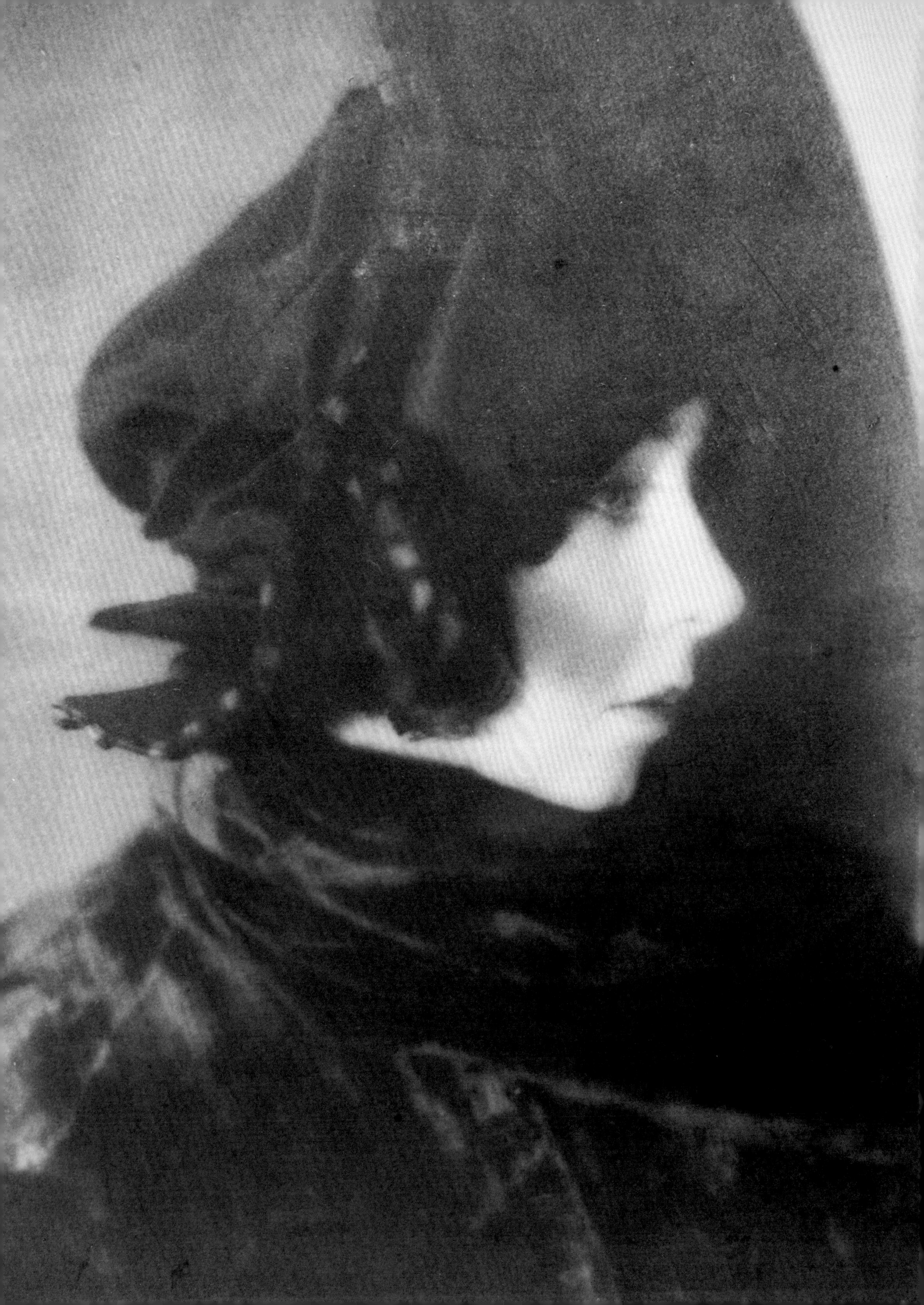

Ethel Wallace

MODERN REBEL

Tara Kaufman

WITH CONTRIBUTIONS BY
Joniah Johnson and Michael Mamp

JAMES A. MICHENER ART MUSEUM
DOYLESTOWN, PENNSYLVANIA

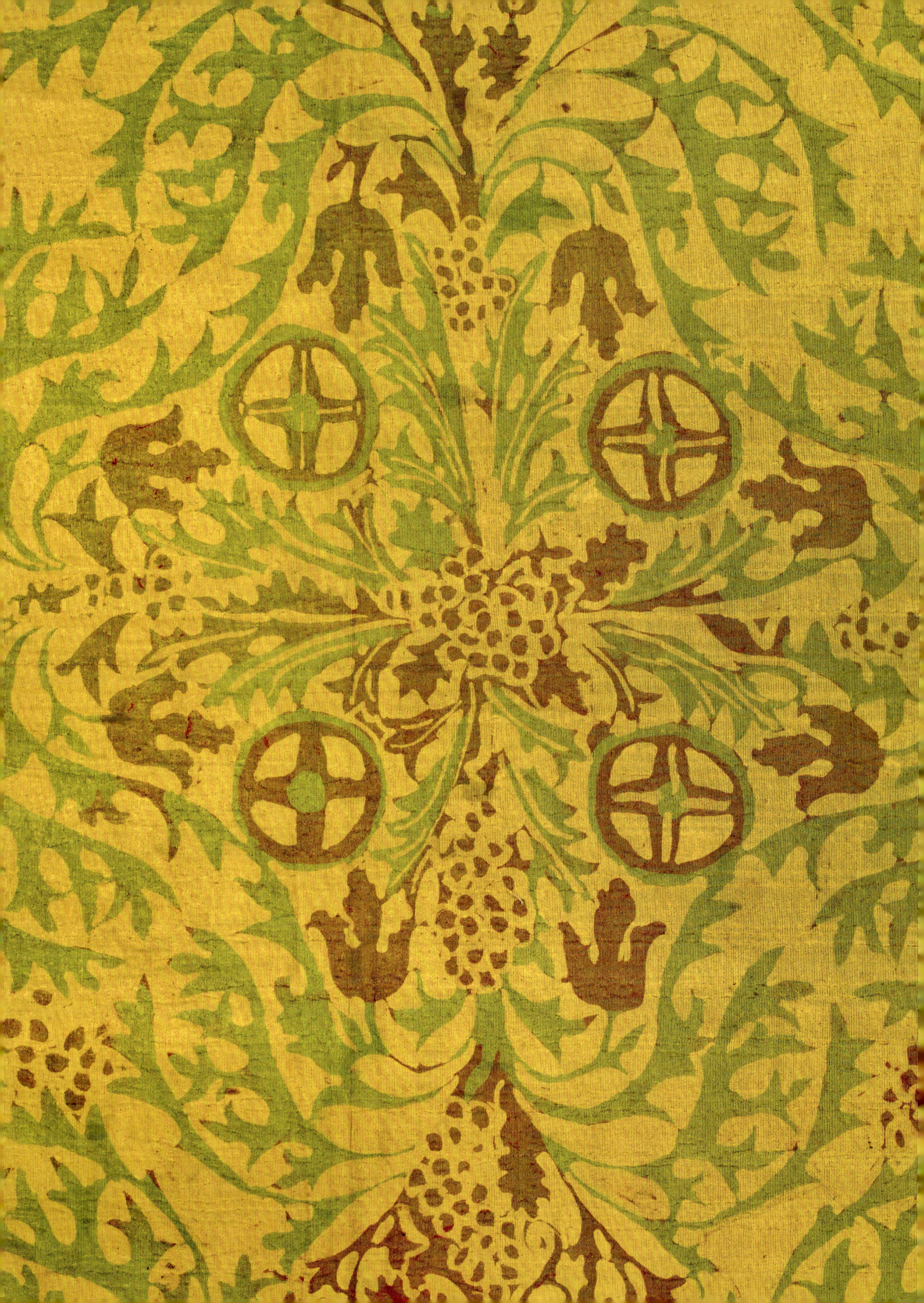

Contents

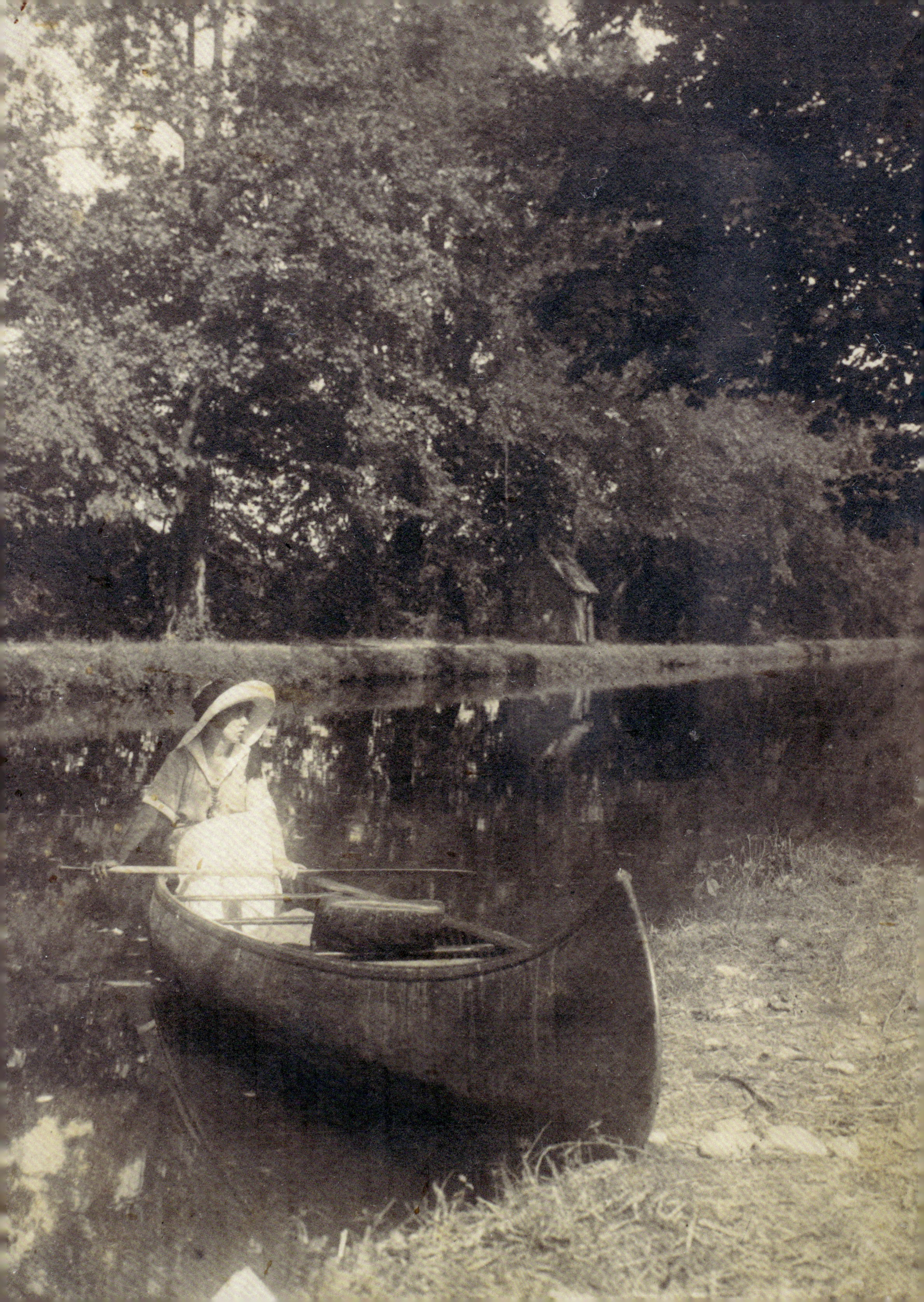

Foreword

NEW HOPE, PENNSYLVANIA, and its environs have long been a haven for artists. Most scholarship on the painters, sculptors, and craftspeople who called this region home, however, has focused on men, like Edward Redfield, William Langson Lathrop, Daniel Garber, Robert Spencer, Rae Sloan Bredin, and John Folinsbee. These artists have all been honored with solo exhibitions of their work at the James A. Michener Art Museum, an honor not paid to any historical woman artist besides Fern Coppedge. We are therefore thrilled to present *Ethel Wallace: Modern Rebel* during the museum's thirty-fifth anniversary year, to help correct this lacuna and further our commitment to highlighting the achievements of women artists from the greater Delaware Valley.

Ethel Wallace: Modern Rebel showcases the work of a previously overlooked artist who achieved success painting fanciful batik portraits and designs in the early twentieth century. As exhibition curator Tara Kaufman writes in her essay, Wallace studied with William Lathrop at Phillips' Mill and, like many of her male contemporaries, enrolled at the Pennsylvania Academy of the Fine Arts. She initially painted in the impressionist style of her teachers Lathrop and Henry McCarter, but her move to New York City connected her with a heady, avant-garde art scene, as she socialized with Joseph Stella, Gertrude Whitney, John Sloan, Walter Arensberg, and others. Her style became more abstract and colorful, and she mixed motifs and designs from different cultures and chronologies in her textiles. She spent the last decades of her life back in Lambertville, New Jersey, working in her father's former grist mill and exhibiting with the New Group, a collective of modernists. She was, until the end, a wildly creative and independent person, devoted to her cats and garden, and experimental in her embrace of different techniques and styles. This exhibition and catalogue recapture her place within the history of the New Hope colony and New York modernism, introducing work that has never before been on public view.

Ethel Wallace: Modern Rebel would not have been possible without the tireless efforts of Jeniah Johnson and her mother, Kristina Barbara Johnson, who preserved Wallace's archives, paintings, and batiks and campaigned for her recognition. Fashion historian Dr. Michael Mamp laid the groundwork for reestablishing Wallace's place within the innovative realm of 1920s fashion and textile design, and we are grateful for his participation in this project and contribution to the catalogue. Wallace could have found no better advocate for her work and story than Tara Kaufman, who spent months immersed in her archives, reading aloud the artist's dramatic correspondence and cat-themed writings. Tara's essay in this catalogue assertively claims a place for Wallace in early modernist art history.

We are thankful for the support of our generous exhibition and catalogue sponsors, including the Richard C. von Hess Foundation, Jeniah Johnson and Tom Sheeran, and the Coby Foundation. Thank you also to our lenders for allowing us to share their paintings and textiles with our visitors, and to the Michener staff who have seen this project to fruition. We hope you will enjoy learning about Wallace, her colorful personality, her exuberant art, and her place within the vibrant arts communities of New Hope and New York.

Laura Turner Igoe
Chief Curator
James A. Michener Art Museum

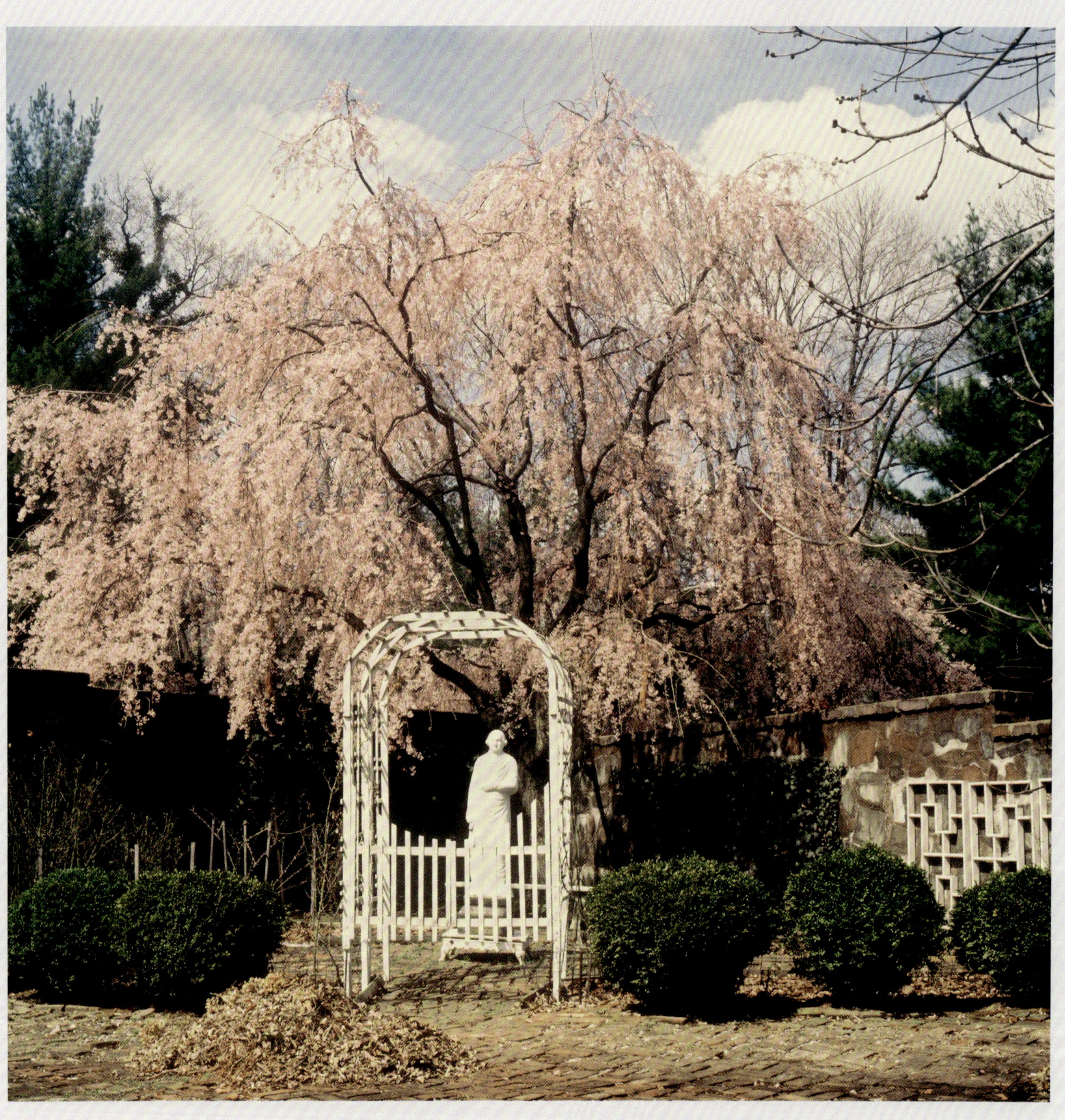

Remembering Ethel

Jeniah (Kookie) Johnson

WHEN I WAS A YOUNG GIRL, I often accompanied my mother, Kristina Barbara Johnson, on her visits to Ethel Wallace's home in New Hope, Pennsylvania. An art collector, my mother admired Ethel's work, and helped support the artist in her old age. To my delight, Ethel had many cats, which kept me occupied while the two women chatted over tea in Ethel's parlor for entire afternoons, often until the sun began to set.

I remember Ethel's house was sparsely furnished, but her garden brimmed with flowers. One spring, she encouraged my mother and me to take home a sapling born of her weeping cherry. We planted the tiny tree in our front yard in Princeton, New Jersey, where it grew to be so magnificent, people would stop their cars to take photos. It still blooms in the same spot five decades later.

When Ethel died, she bequeathed to my mother her art as well as letters, notebooks, photographs, several chinoiserie treasures, and an enormous carved chest full of batiks and costumes of Ethel's making along with kimonos, gowns, and accessories she'd collected. I spent countless hours playing dress-up with these items, imagining myself a fashionable artist from the Roaring Twenties.

While I could never equal Ethel's style, I was positively influenced by the legacy of this independent woman who defied societal constraints in order to learn, travel, and make art. I am deeply grateful to Tara Kaufman and the Michener Art Museum for recognizing Ethel's talent and important history, and to Michael Mamp, Edwin Hild, and all the historians, collectors, dealers, and friends who hold Ethel close to their hearts.

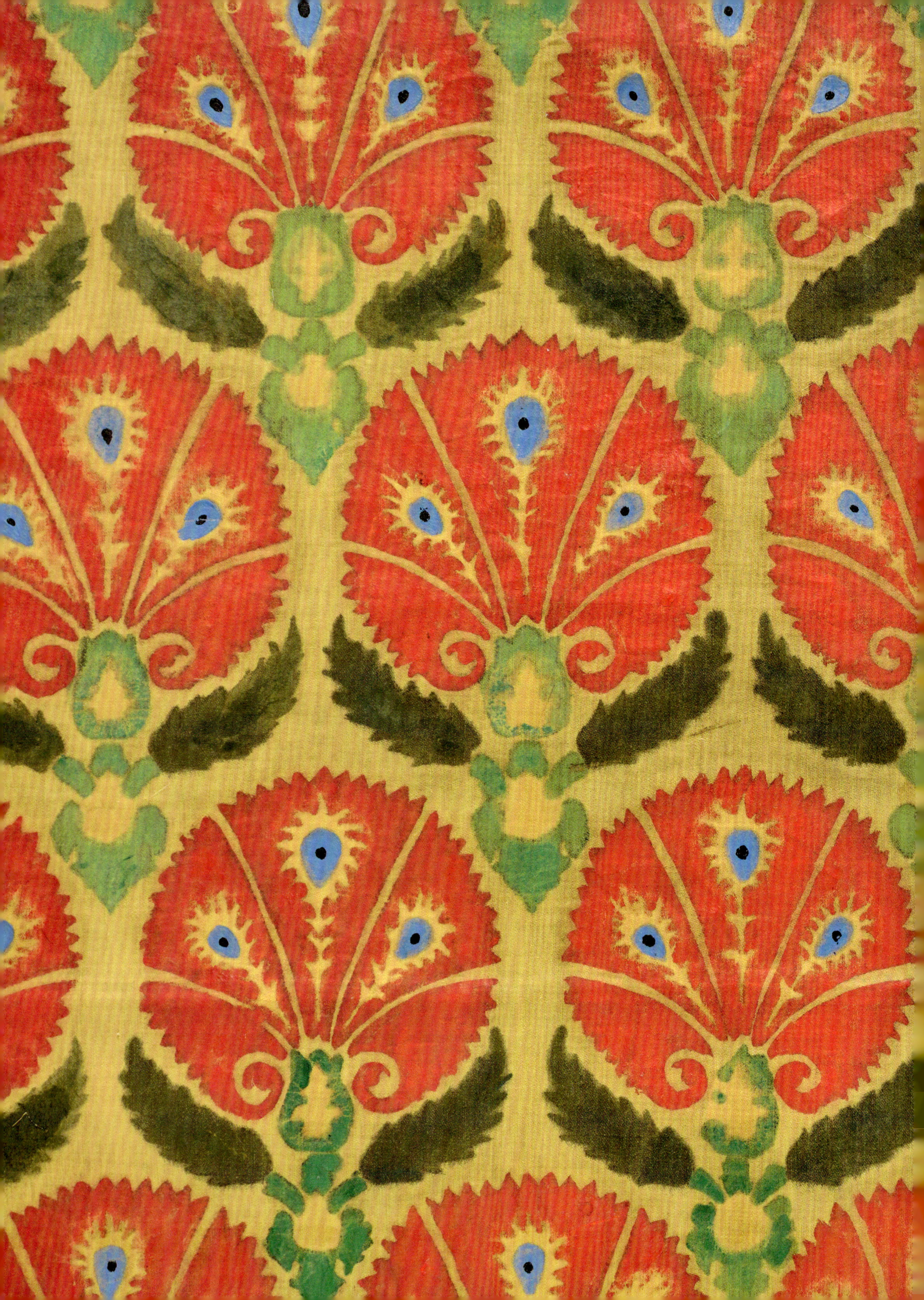

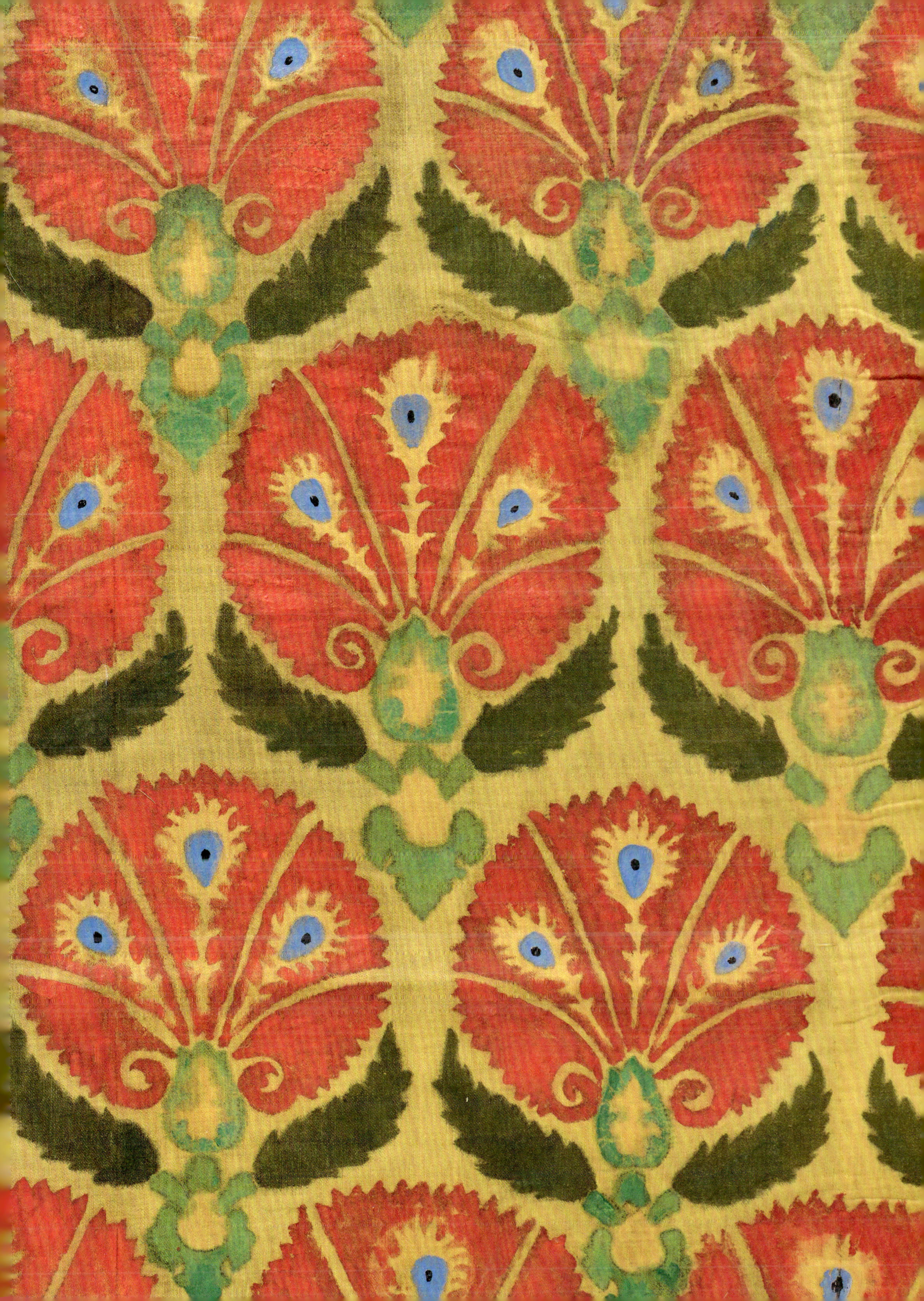

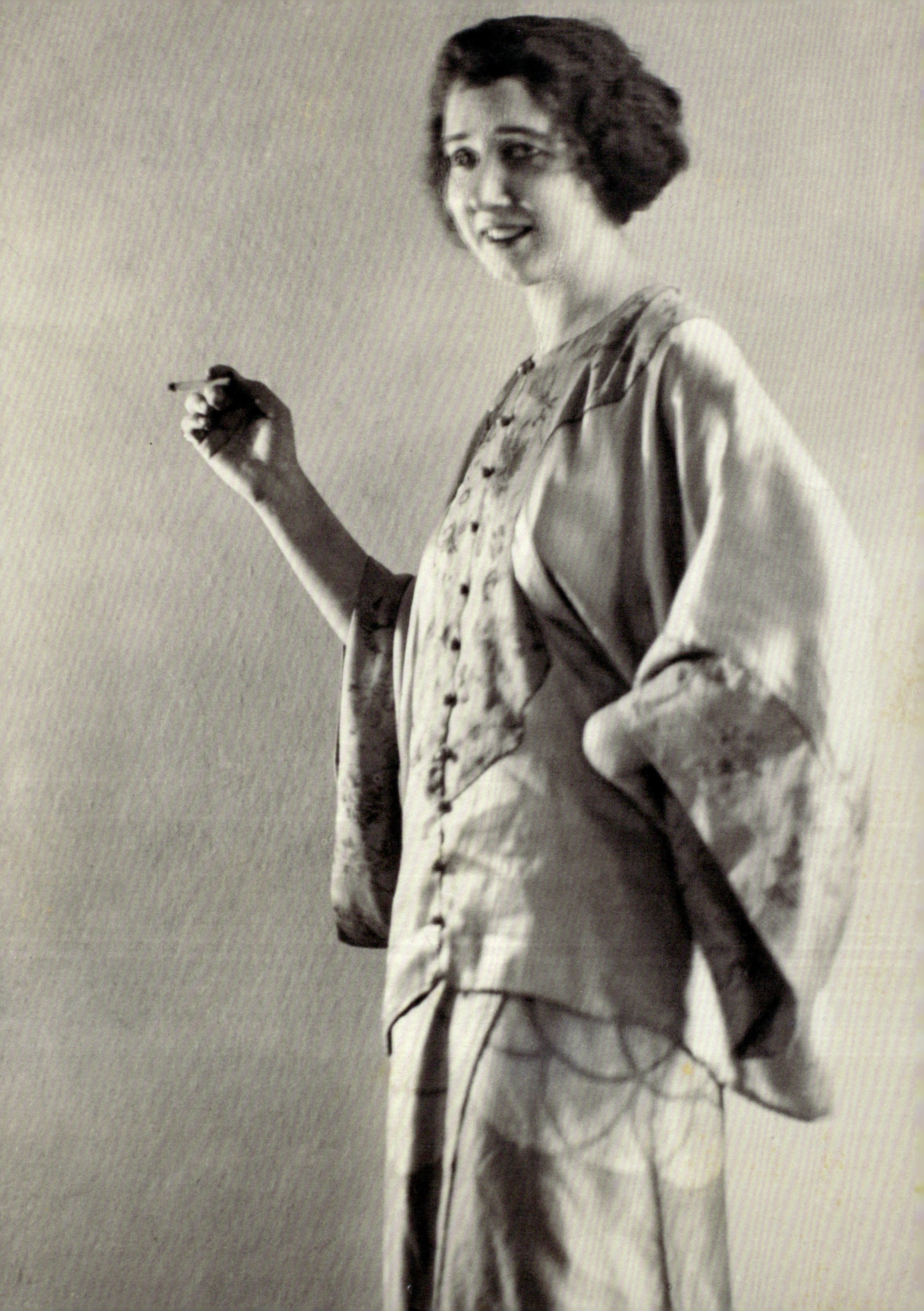

A Modern Rebel

Tara Kaufman

I'm going to be charming until the end.

—Ethel Wallace

A HEADLINE PRINTED IN 1968 in the *Bucks County Gazette* reads simply, "Ethel Is Gone."[1] In the same issue, an article written by theater producer Mike Ellis, a close friend of artist Ethel Wallace (1886–1968), laments the loss of a woman who in life had been an enchanting and beloved figure in the community.[2] Ethel's "magic," as he put it on a postcard written to her in her last months, was something one could "catch" simply by spending time with her.[3] Born in Recklesstown (now Chesterfield Township), New Jersey, in 1886, Wallace grew up in the artistic community of New Hope, Pennsylvania, before moving to New York City and building a sensational reputation and successful business as a textile artist and fashion designer. But her career in New York was cut short when her textile shop burned down, prompting her return to New Hope. The Great Depression ensured she stayed. For the remainder of her life, she embedded herself in the community, which in turn exalted her as a Bucks County eccentric. Ethel, however, belonged to no one. She was a fiercely independent entrepreneur and whip-smart modern woman who enjoyed romantic relationships with multiple partners and refused to limit her life to domesticity.[4] Her work—from her writings to her paintings and clothing designs—traces the development of two centers of modernism in the United States—New Hope and New York—while the trajectory of her career brings into focus the complications that faced a woman, even an intrepid one, working as an artist during the culturally transformative eras through which she lived.

Ethel is, inarguably, gone. She rests beneath a headstone of the same uniform shape and size as the hundreds that surround her, in a Quaker graveyard located just down the street from the house in which she lived her final years. Only a mile away are the homes of the late, celebrated Pennsylvania impressionist William Langson Lathrop, with whom Wallace trained as a young child, and Eleanor Miller, a musical theater actress and daughter-in-law of New Hope artist R. A. D. Miller. Eleanor has recounted to me treasured memories from her own childhood of visiting Wallace: in her words, Wallace was "a love."[5] Another friend, Brenda Meredith, frequently visited Wallace shortly before her death in 1968 and, despite the decades that have passed, still remembers that Wallace spoke colorfully of the people she'd known and kept her home open to company and warm with the purring of cats.[6] To the community of Bucks County, Wallace is a legend. People speak of her sneaking through her neighbors' windows in the middle of the night to deliver her coveted lemon butter or driving around town without a windshield, either because she didn't have the money to fix it or because she didn't care. Wallace's writings contain the same wit with which she is described, but they also reflect her deep connection to the natural world and the place where she was raised. In one note, she writes, "I see only the big river flowing to the edge of heaven—this theme in so many of my decorations— this preoccupation with the movement of a river—so much childhood spent in watching the Delaware—that moment of leaning over the Pont— bridge—watching the reflection of the moon." One can picture her there: out on her own at midnight, leaning over the edge of a bridge just to watch the water scatter the moonlight, thinking of form, abstraction, and movement, and how to translate them in paint.

Wallace's early work caught the impressionist wave that first hit the United States in the late nineteenth and early twentieth centuries, when she was a young artist in New Hope and Philadelphia. In her childhood, her father, Winfield Wallace, operated a grist mill in Lambertville, New Jersey, a small town separated from New Hope by only a narrow strip of the Delaware River. Two early paintings, *River Bridge (New Hope)* and *Untitled (Delaware Canal Scene)* (Figs. 1 and 2), capture the charm of these countryside towns in lush, warm greens and yellows rendered with the brushy texture of impressionism, first made famous in this region by her mentor, William Lathrop (Fig. 3). After he established his studio at Phillips' Mill, a historic eighteenth-century residence located alongside the Delaware Canal, Lathrop's reputation as a nationally recognized artist, as well as that of fellow local artist Edward Redfield, drew other artists to Bucks County. With his wife, Annie, Lathrop supported the emerging artistic community through classes and social gatherings held at their home, which became known for their famous Sunday teas.[7] In addition to Wallace's time learning from Lathrop, she continued her studies with colorist Henry McCarter at the Pennsylvania Academy of the Fine Arts, in Philadelphia. A fantastical painting by McCarter from this era, titled *Symphony* (Fig. 4), limns mystical and medieval imagery in a vibrant, graphic style that could have influenced Wallace's later, modern approach to

FIG. 1
Ethel Wallace (1886–1968), *River Bridge
(New Hope)*, ca. 1911. Oil on canvas, 32 ×
24 inches. Jim's of Lambertville, New
Jersey.

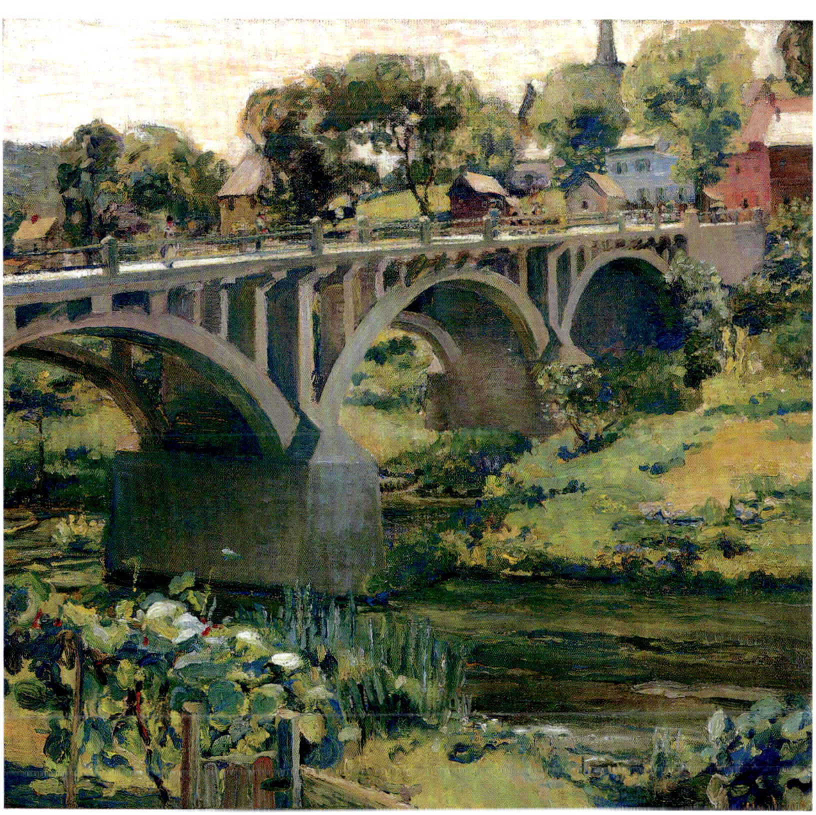

FIG. 2
Ethel Wallace (1886–1968), *Untitled
(Delaware Canal Scene)*, ca. 1910. Oil on
canvas, 36 × 40 inches (framed). Collection of Sue Bunkin.

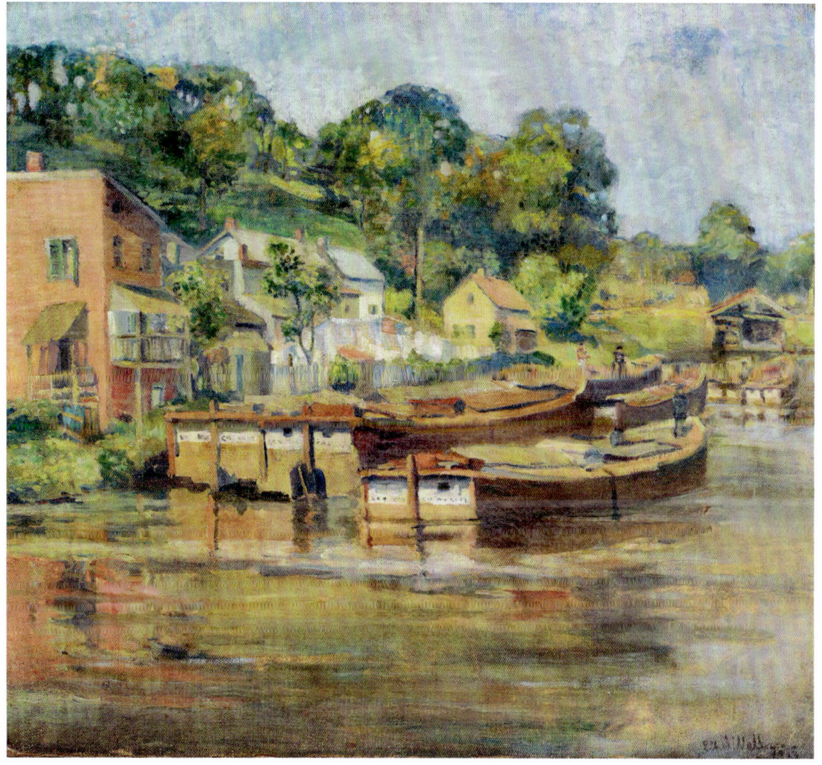

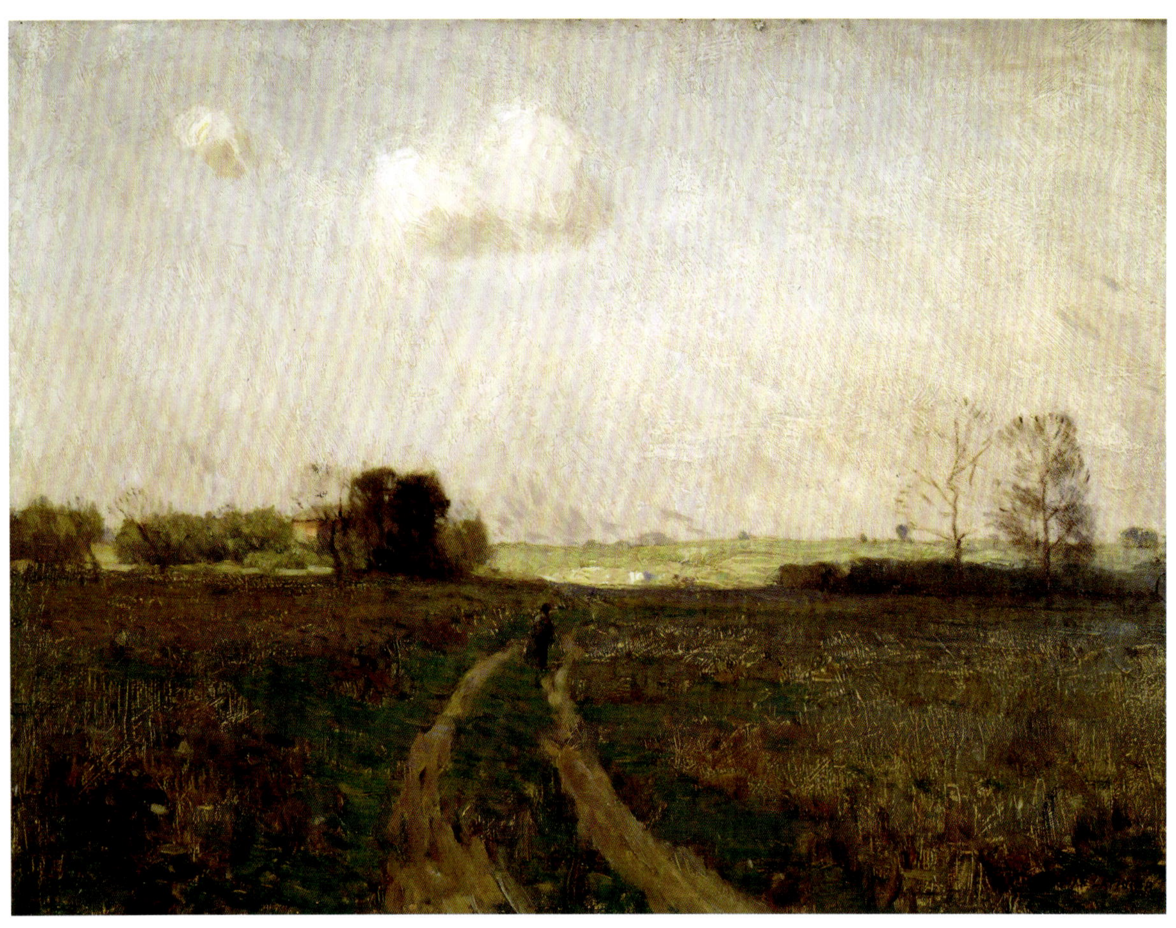

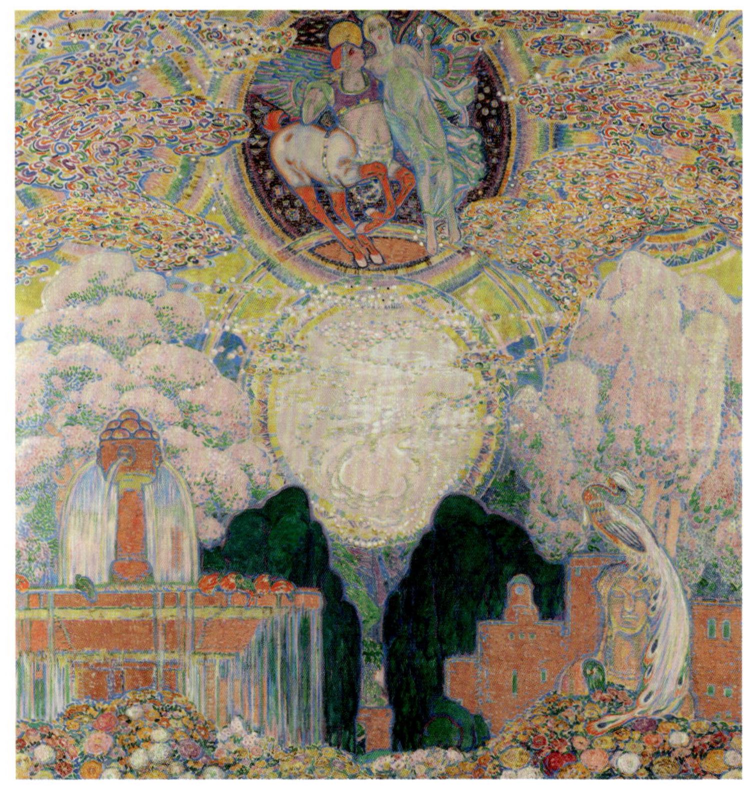

FIG. 3
William Langson Lathrop (1859–1938),
Untitled (Landscape with Figure),
ca. 1897. Oil on canvas, 19 × 25 inches.
James A. Michener Art Museum,
Michener Art Endowment Challenge,
Gift of Malcolm and Eleanor Polis,
1993.2.

FIG. 4
Henry McCarter (1864–1942), *Symphony*, by 1915. Oil on canvas, 103⅜ × 100⅝ inches. Pennsylvania Academy of the Fine Arts, Philadelphia, Gift of Mrs. Henry Clifford, 1944.33.

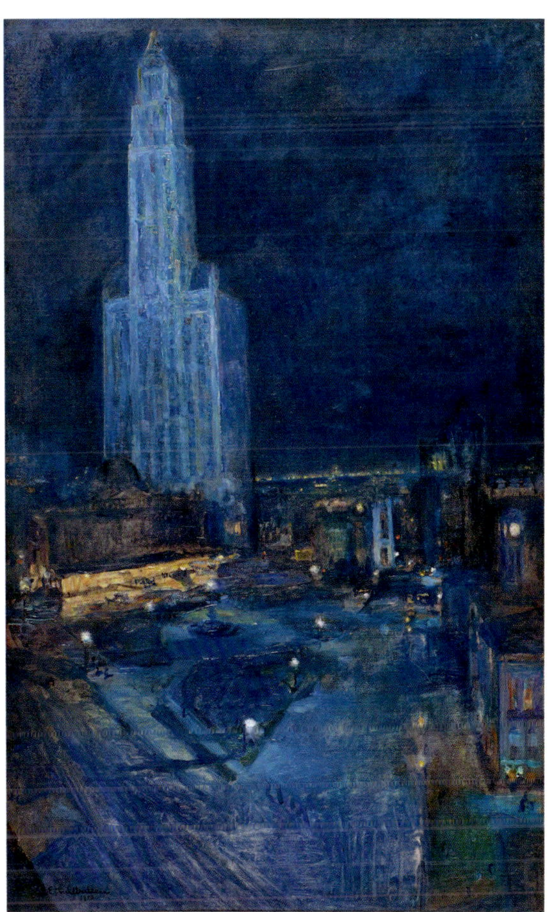

medieval artwork. While these years of study were critical to her adaptation of the broken brushwork style of painting that she would later return to, it was her break from these teachers and techniques that opened a space for her to innovate and find her own place in the American art scene.

The move to New York City was pivotal. Within her first few years there, Wallace would witness the groundbreaking 1913 Armory Show, marry and separate from her husband, participate in the women's suffrage movement and see its success, and befriend and exchange ideas with modernists whose work would radically transform her own. In a 1913 moonlight view of the newly constructed Woolworth Building, moody blue, nostalgic light enshrouds the tower (Fig. 5). Its ghostly shape juts into a starry sky— nearly disappearing into space—and looms over the glowing square below, evoking wonder and unease.[8] The composition charts the tower's impact on the city's skyline and signals a shift from Wallace's go-to sentimental countryside views to a more contemplative study of the changing urban environments in which she lived. Upon its completion, the Woolworth set the record for the world's tallest building; earlier that same year, the city's Grand Central Terminal had opened. Landmarks like these, built using steel and equipped with electricity to meet the demands of a booming economy and a growing population, served as symbols of the country's rapid industrialization and increasing power.[9] Like John Sloan's hazy nighttime view of New York's urban landscape and the distant Woolworth (Fig. 6), Wallace's depiction of the skyscraper envelops its brutal interruption of the landscape in softer atmospheric light, romance, and mystery.

The dizzying representations of the Brooklyn Bridge painted obsessively by Italian American futurist Joseph Stella captured the might and energy of the modern landscape and struck a chord with Wallace, who befriended Stella and painted his portrait (Figs. 7 and 8). Posed in the painting with a cigarette in hand and color beaming over him like sunlight, Stella sits against a background rife with motifs found in his intricate bridge and nature paintings. Wallace's composition embraces the dynamic new age with contrasting color and clashing planes but nearly overwhelms the sharp skyline with flowing, organic imagery. Lithe swans swim and encircle a female nude, whose sinuous form and dreamy movements are characteristic of Wallace's signature figures and evoke Florine Stettheimer's stylized figures (Fig. 9). Whether Wallace knew of Stettheimer or of her work is unknown, but in that smoke-clouded social era of New York, it is very possible that she attended one of Stettheimer's famed salons. After all, Wallace had already harnessed her charming personality to make a place for herself in the city's avant-garde circles. She exhibited with the Society of Independent Artists, founded in 1917 to

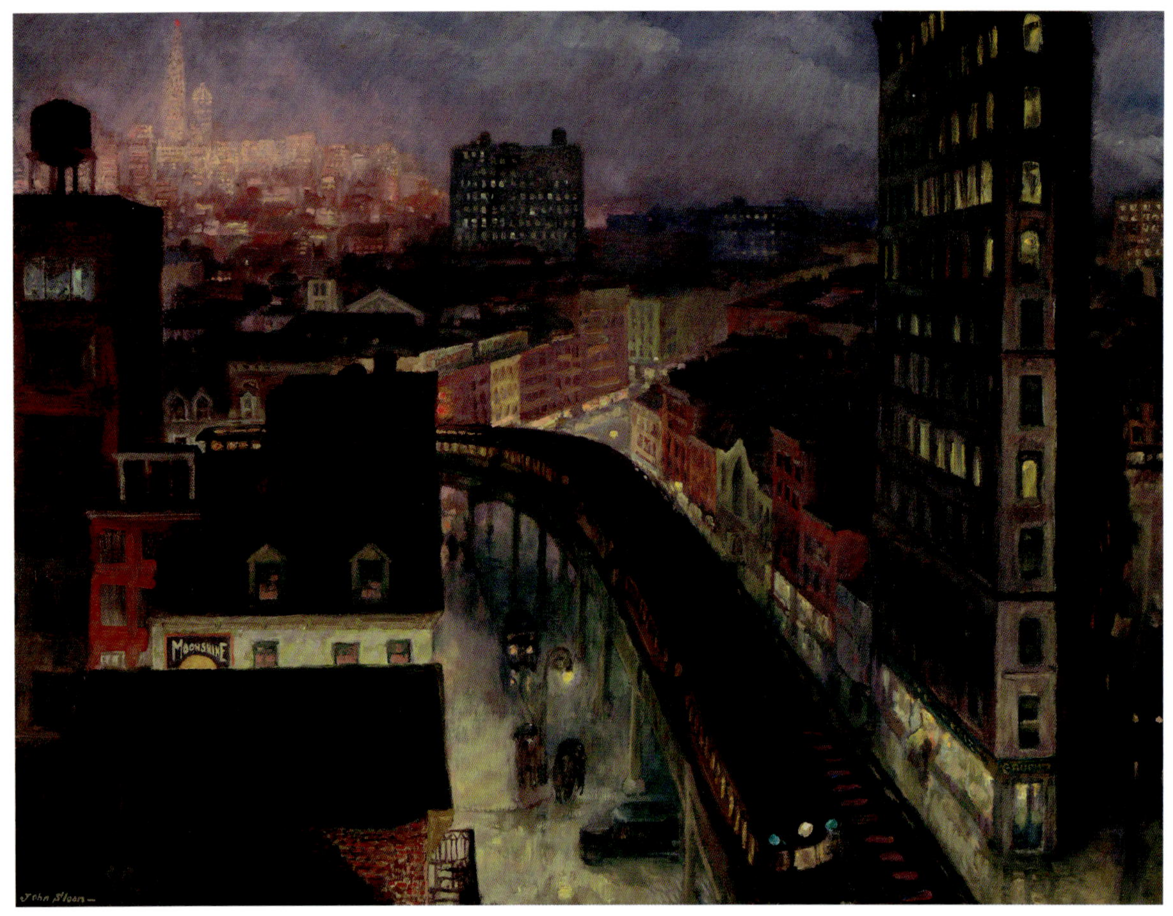

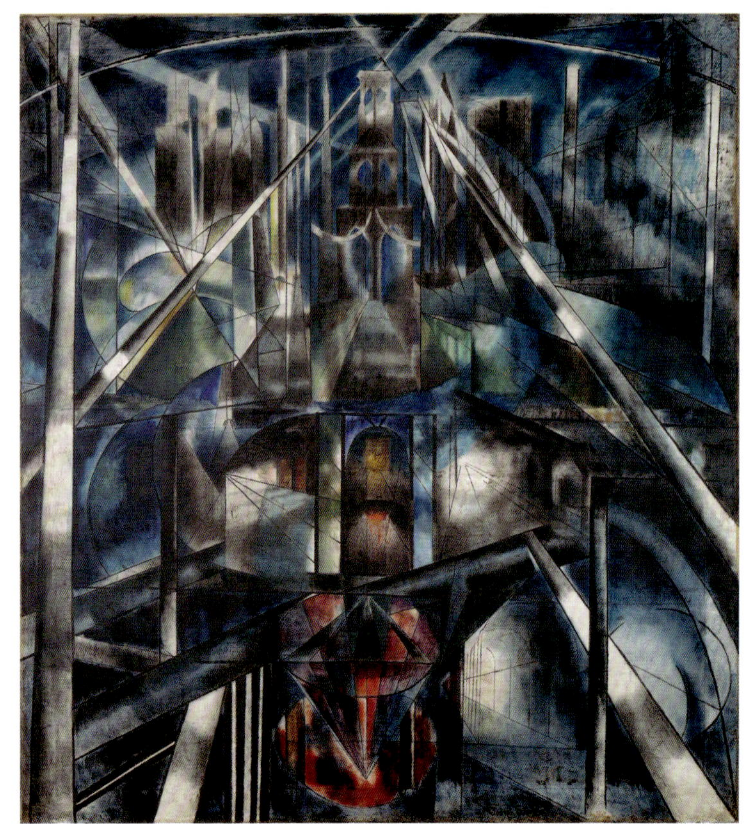

FIG. 6
John Sloan (1871–1951), *The City from Greenwich Village*, 1922. Oil on canvas, 26 × 33¾ inches. Collection of the National Gallery of Art, Washington, DC, Gift of Helen Farr Sloan, 1970.1.1.

FIG. 7
Joseph Stella (1877–1946), *Brooklyn Bridge*, 1919–20. Oil on canvas, 84¾ × 76⅜ inches. Yale University Art Gallery, New Haven, Connecticut, Gift of Collection Société Anonyme, 1941.690.

FIG. 8
Ethel Wallace (1886–1968), *Portrait of Joseph Stella*, ca. 1920. Oil on canvas, 69 × 44 inches. Collection of the late Kristina Barbara Johnson, courtesy of Jeniah Johnson.

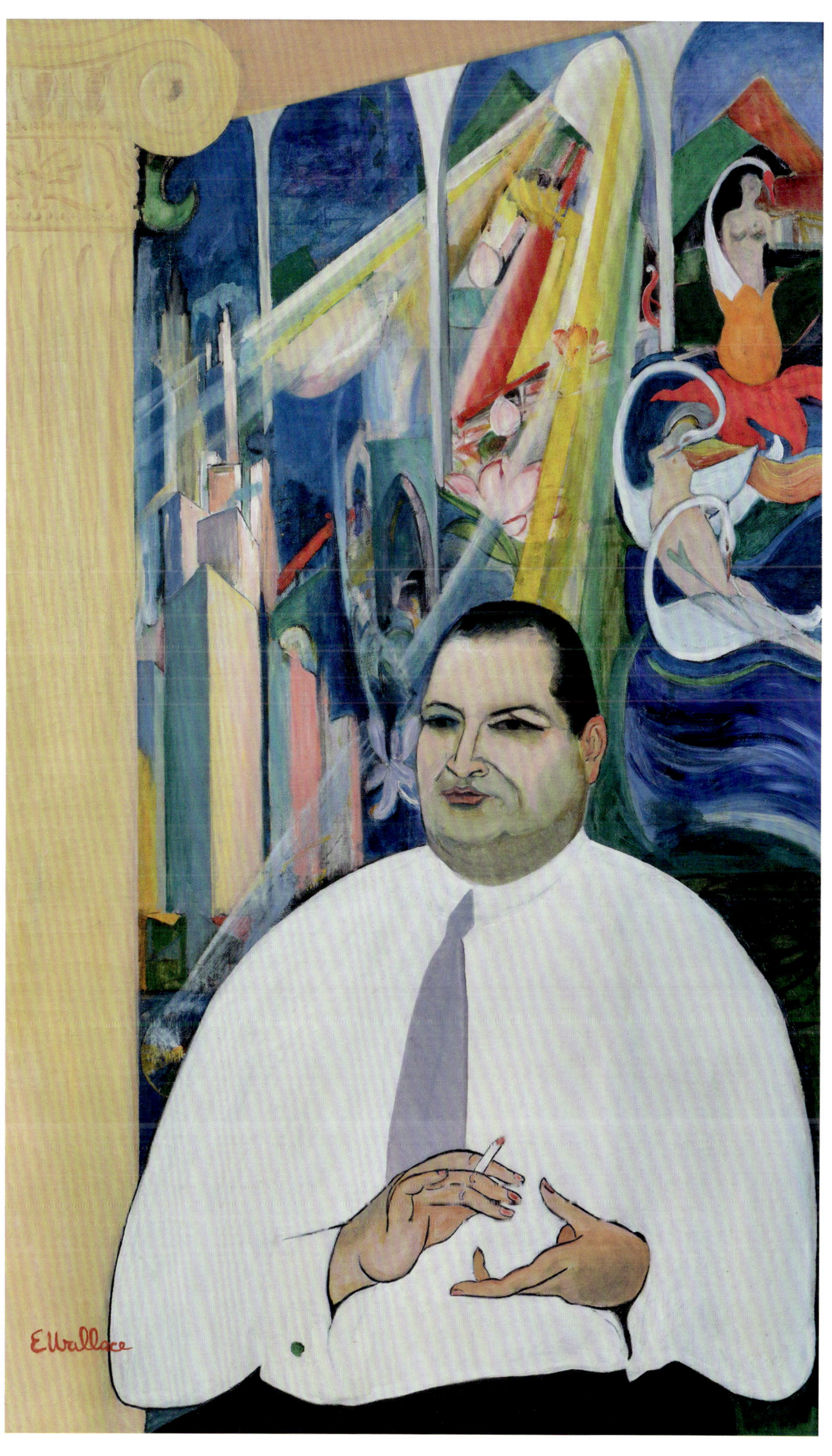

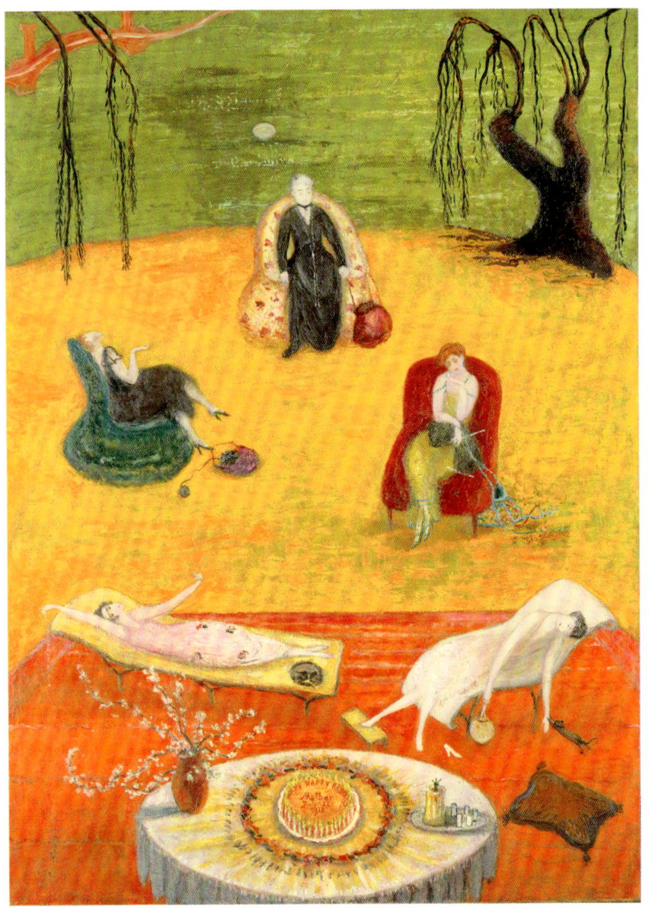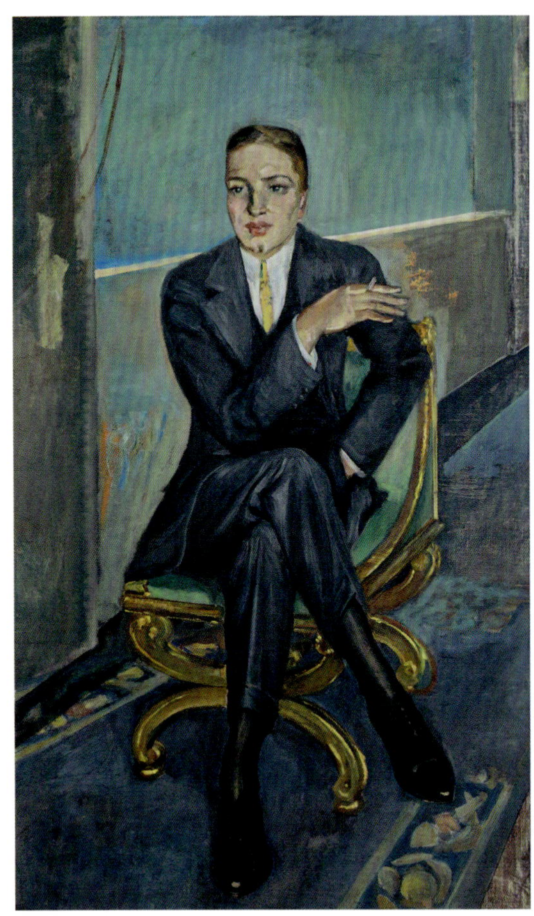

allow artists to exhibit their work no matter how modern or eccentric the content; and her address books, which list popular social spots and names like Gertrude Whitney, Juliana Force, John Sloan, and Walter Arensberg, elicit images of spirited conversations held in dark bars and parties crowded into glittering Roaring Twenties rooms.[10] She evidently painted portraits of many of her friends, frequently posed with the requisite cigarette (Fig. 10). Her portrait of Stella, in which she scrapped her soft pastels for a brighter, fauvist palette and sharp, simplified forms, attests to her involvement in an art scene and movement now recognized as historic.

Despite her marked shift from impressionism to modernism, few paintings made in this bright, abstracted style are known to exist in Wallace's body of work. Throughout the early 1910s, she continued to exhibit traditional landscapes, though in venues that were distinctly progressive. In 1915, she used her work to advocate for women's rights by contributing a painting to an exhibition benefiting suffrage efforts.

SAUCE FOR THE GANDER AND THE GOOSE

The *Exhibition of Painting and Sculpture by Women Artists for the Benefit of the Woman Suffrage Campaign* was held at New York City's prestigious Macbeth Gallery from September 27 through October 17, 1915, with half the proceeds from sales directed toward the Empire State Suffrage Campaign.[11] Ninety women contributed more than 150 works to the show, with subjects ranging from explicitly feminist imagery, as in Theresa Bernstein's painting *The Suffrage Meeting* (1914), to traditional genres like landscape painting.[12] Wallace's contribution, a now-lost painting titled *In the Village* (n.d.), likely fell into this latter category. Though the exhibition was criticized for works like Wallace's that didn't capture pro-suffrage sentiments or displayed only maternal and domestic subject matter, historian Laura Prieto argues that "by contributing work and consenting to appear in the catalogue, each of the artists publicly and undeniably declared herself allied with the movement," and in turn, the meaning of the works—no matter the subject—changed.[13] A simple landscape of a village, in this case, belies the ambition behind it: it was a work informed by professional training only recently available to women, painted with a confidence that it could compete with work made by men, and exhibited to advocate for women's right to determine the political future of the country.

Wallace herself was outspoken and opinionated, and her feminism permeated every aspect of her life and work. By the time she arrived in New York, she was twenty-six years old and sharply aware of the barriers that had been built to hold her back. Scrawled on the scraps of the aged pages that now comprise her papers are clipped thoughts like "she [found] herself against the wall of a male education" and "what is sauce for the gander is sauce for the goose—she regarded herself as equally free [as men]." In the decades before Wallace began her career, women artists had already begun dismantling societal expectations confining women's work to domesticity by asserting their status as professionals. Between the 1890s and 1920s, an era of social and political activism known as the Progressive Era, women gained access to education, formed networks and women's artist groups, and created opportunities to exhibit their work either alongside or independent from artwork made by men.[14] Those who married found the need to balance their dual roles as wife and artist, and for a time, Wallace did the same.

In 1912, her marriage to Nathaniel "Nat" Fielding Roberts, an engineer for the American Telephone and Telegraph Company, enclosed her in a domestic role she found stifling. Between her desire to pursue her career, her struggle to find happiness in her new marriage, and Roberts's frequent travels abroad for work, the two eventually separated. Later, describing the sense of duty she felt in her marriage, Wallace wrote, "Oh the emotional existence like that is horrible, horrible I was never myself—I was stupid tongue-tied I dropped all my tricks of personality— I was a thing—And I thought it would endure forever."[15] In another note (in which she could not resist comparing herself to one of her beloved cats), she wrote, "She treated men as a cat that lived [with] a person would. Curling against their shoulder, remote as to marriage. She would not or could not understand the female jargon of cozy domesticity. Split level houses, things in cans—was it the dull language—images it called up like the sterile quality of an operating room—quite proper in its place."[16]

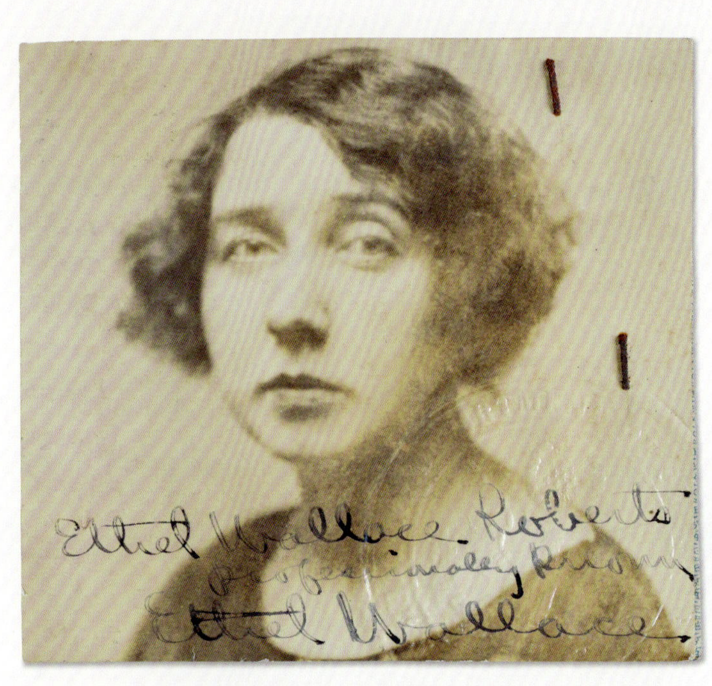

Free from her responsibilities as a wife, Wallace dropped her married name and, as one photo shows, very pointedly reminded others of her professional name, Ethel Wallace (Fig. 11). An article glued to a page in one of her many scrapbooks ties her actions to a larger national trend:

> Why should any one have thought that women would stop with the acquisition of the vote? The moment is perhaps here for the beginning of the attempt to win men's rights. One of the most agreeably sensational features of metropolitan life this season is the band of ladies who entirely decline, upon marriage, to become Mrs. Smith, Brown, or Green, but insist upon being known still as Miss Jones, White, or Farquharson as their original appellations were. . . . The argument on the side of the rebels is a pretty obvious one, and the obvious argument is apt to be a strong one. There is no longer any way of combating the idea that no woman should by marriage lose her individuality, lose her own individual chance of being honored for her achievement, merge herself into her husband's life and work.[17]

Reproduced front and center on the page is a portrait by Wallace—a quirky interpretation of the unmarried American playwright and socialite Mary Hoyt Wiborg—identifying the artist and her subject with the rebels and linking her work to advancements in women's rights, professionalism, and independence (Fig. 12).

THE REVIEWING STAND

By HARRISON RHODES

WHY should any one have thought that women would stop with the acquisition of the vote? The moment is perhaps here for the beginning of the attempt to win men's rights. One of the most agreeably sensational features of metropolitan life this season is the band of ladies who entirely decline, upon marriage, to become Mrs. Smith, Brown, or Green, but insist upon being known still as Miss Jones, White, or Farquharson as their original appellations were. There was, it appears, in the Nineteenth Century of women's slavery to men an intrepid early feminist named, was she not? Miss Lucy Stone. She secured a husband—an unusual achievement for a woman's rights woman in those days (if the fact may be pointed out without rancor), but she remained Stone. Her very name is now the badge of revolution, the club circle of the elect bears her name. She is saint or pro-martyr or something like that of the advancing female tide. And if you do not venerate her, you must admit that she and her followers have propounded a very interesting question.

The argument on the side of the rebels is a pretty obvious one, and the obvious argument is apt to be a strong one. There is no longer any way of combating the idea that no woman should by marriage lose her individuality, lose her own individual chance of being honored for her achievement, merge herself into her husband's life and work. And it is obvious that there is no woman but runs a risk, after she has begun a career, if she changes her name—first by marriage or later by divorce.

To speak of the possibility of divorce so lightly is in no sense nowadays to be disillusioned. So common is the breaking of ties that no young woman of the kind in question here can marry nowadays without the possibility of a loosening of the tie crossing her mind almost at the very altar. Indeed, it is amusing to find that among the most ardent advocates of "one name forever" there are two widely contrasting opinions. One party holds that to keep one's name will enormously facilitate divorce by removing the embarrassing, almost comic, changes of nomenclature, which might make women hesitate. Husbands will be, according to this school of thought, mere varying flotsam upon the great current of a woman's life, the occasional diversion, as it were, of her hours of ease. Those who disagree say that if by granting a woman full scope the husband is reduced to the position of an appurtenance, used mainly for paternity purposes, he will become so comparatively unimportant that it will scarcely be worth while changing him often. Both parties are agreed at least in relegating the consort of a modern woman to a position where he cannot disturb the calm of her domestic happiness.

It is the privilege of anyone in the full cry of metropolitan life to observe a certain number of these *menages*. And it is only fair to say that they present a great appearance of success. The husbands are bright and in excellent physical condition, and in many cases have found occupations of their own which please them and fill their time and even enable them to contribute, if only modestly, to the family exchequer.

THERE is, it is understood, one matter of dissension, which still disturbs some of these new alliances: shall the child (or children) take the name of the mother or that of the father (or fathers)? There is here undoubtedly an opportunity for several of what are termed in the vernacular "wise cracks." They shall not be made, for there is a certain decorum of *The Reviewing Stand* and in fact it is difficult to discern any general guiding principle to which it is easy to subscribe which would solve the problem. Doubtless in the mediæval debates upon the Salic Law there may have been

something which would now shed light. But the ordinary modern investigator sees only that whereas it was once an honor for a child to bear its father's name it is now a greater one to bear its mother's. The whole matter must be subject of lively and interesting debates which it would be a pleasure to hear, among the progenitors concerned. Perhaps all that can be said is, let the best parents win. Unless the Spanish method can be adopted and the little daughter of John Smith and Mary Jones be known as little Miss Doris Smith-y-Jones.

Mary Jones is ordinarily known as Miss Mary Jones. And here issue is taken with the Lucy Stoneists. We *do* somehow wish that it might be Mrs. Mary Jones who was living with Mr. John Smith, not Miss Jones. It would give the innocent public some kind of an inkling that some kind of a legal formality sanctioning some kind of a union had been gone through. Not of course that it would give the hotel clerk where the pair registered quite enough to go upon in any case. Hotel clerks, it is said, still live in full Nineteenth Century morality. They see no reason why Mr. Smith should be assigned a room with either Mrs. or Miss Jones, though quite ready to accept almost anybody if she will only assert that she is Mrs. Smith.

Advocates of double nomenclature admit that such monstrous old-fashioned morality makes it almost easier for the advanced not to travel. And so it may be that the simple hotel clerk is making domesticity perforce flourish more and more around the home hearth.

It would be pleasant, and very modern, to feel that Miss Jones refused at a decent hotel is a martyr. But a possibly too long familiarity with French farces and a rather old-fashioned sense of humor combine to make the poor lady's plight seem rather comic than otherwise.

The same weakness, the same unfortunate Nineteenth Century past keeps one from taking as seriously as it deserves the question of whether the husband should be permitted a domicile under his wife's roof, or should merely visit her at tea time or any other moments (by telephonic appointment, of course), which a romantic and impassioned relationship may demand. In the old days women often wanted to make husbands of their lovers; now they merely want to make lovers of their husbands. And there is a great deal to be said on their side. That their activities seem to some of us merely to be the raw material for delightful fantastic comedy is perhaps not an argument against them.

IS it a sign of mere callousness or of coming age that it is becoming increasingly difficult to sympathize as one would, as a gentleman, wish to, with the heroines of plays? Your humble servant of *The Reviewing Stand* has perhaps had a run of theatrical bad luck lately. He has seen upon the stage an undue number of ladies whose happiness was painfully prevented by geographical isolation, by lack of money, by unsympathetic husbands who seemed to demand work and the sharing of difficulties from their helpmates. Of course, if in the audience you can let yourself go on the full tide of emotion, if crystal drops coursing down the actress' lovely cheek sympathetically stimulate your own tear-ducts all is well. But if you stop to analyze the situation of these unhappy females, you will be forced to see that they all really are martyrized because they cannot be in Fifth Avenue in limousine cars stopping to buy expensive lingerie. They talk about the development of their souls, but what they really mean is that they want silk stockings.

They are very true and symptomatic of the times, when luxury and idleness are all, it would appear, that anyone anywhere wants. But are we to be very sorry about them? Fifth Avenue would be *(Continued on page 72)*

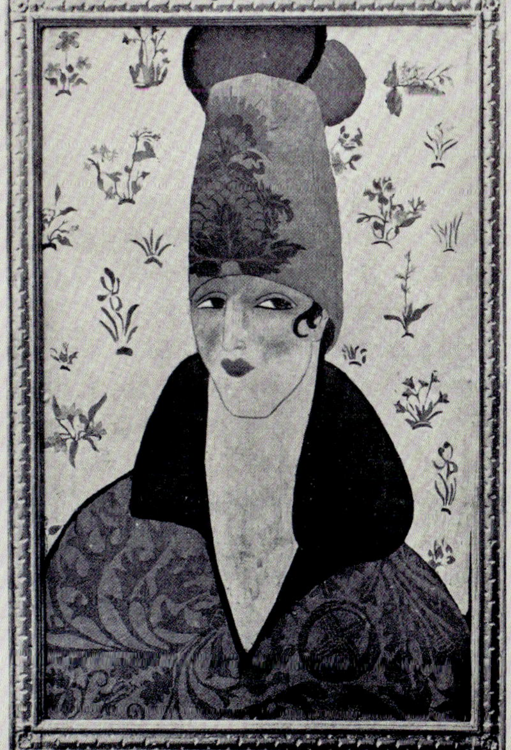

Courtesy of the Kingore Gallery

MISS MARY HOYT WIBORG

From a fanciful portrait, dyed on silk, by Ethel Wallace, a young American of much personality, who has had a genuine artistic success with her "paintings" on silk both in London and America. Miss Wallace has most recently been having exhibitions in Boston and Chicago

Though she continued to exhibit her work, in the absence of consistent production or critical reception of either her impressionistic landscapes or her abstracted, moody cityscapes, Wallace evidently felt pressure to conform to the latest trends in modernism. She later complained in a letter about people's expectations for her work: she wrote, as if imitating their comments, "Would I please stop being curved & snap into modern straight lines—if other things changed with steel & new metals, new shapes, so should emotions & ideas."[18] Not one to bend to the will of others, Wallace embraced her own ideas and "curved lines" and developed a style that quite literally made women shine, using gilt panels and swaths of silk and velvet painted with free-flowing lines and lush foliage. The works resonated with glamorous women and patrons who found a kinship with Wallace's vision and launched the career she'd been working toward.

SHIMMERING MOONBEAMS AND SONGS OF THE FAIRY FOREST

Wallace's adaptation of batik, a Javanese method of dyeing cloth, evolved along with her production of modern portraits and medieval-style paintings. She expanded on the work of Gilded Age artists who, out of their wariness toward mass production, turned to premodern times and cultures perceived as "primitive" to express a refined, one-of-a-kind aesthetic. Her work took on a decorative quality rich with organic imagery and flowing lines, a style aligned with the Arts and Crafts aesthetic and receptive to the Roaring Twenties obsession with wealth and opulence.[19] An insatiable creative and intellectual, she appropriated motifs and designs from Egyptian, Asian, European, and Mediterranean cultures to find source material for her perpetually evolving style. Three works from this period recall the gilt surfaces of medieval France (Figs. 13–15). The largest, a standing screen, features a narrative scene of a South Asian–inspired woman plucking a lute and surrounded by figures from varying social classes (Fig. 13). In the foreground, those of nobility wear intricately embroidered tunics, chain mail, and symbols of power and faith, including fleurs-de-lis, a hooded falcon, and lions. Her inclusion of the lions likely satisfied her cat infatuation and perhaps referenced a pair of gilt Chinese Foo dogs in her collection as well as her family history; the Wallace family coat of arms consisted of two rearing lions, whose scroll-like fur resembles that of the lions in her screen (Figs. 16 and 17). Despite her wide-ranging source material, Wallace maintained in her medieval paintings the flattened, sinuous forms and bold outlines seen in the decidedly modern portraits she painted on canvas and silk.

One of her medieval-style works, *The Blue Devil*, provides insight into her process of translating oil portraits to batik (Fig. 15). The painting features a soldier from France's Chasseurs alpins (Alpine Hunters), an elite military unit specialized in fighting in mountainous terrain and nicknamed "les Diables bleus" for their skill and blue uniforms.[20] After

26

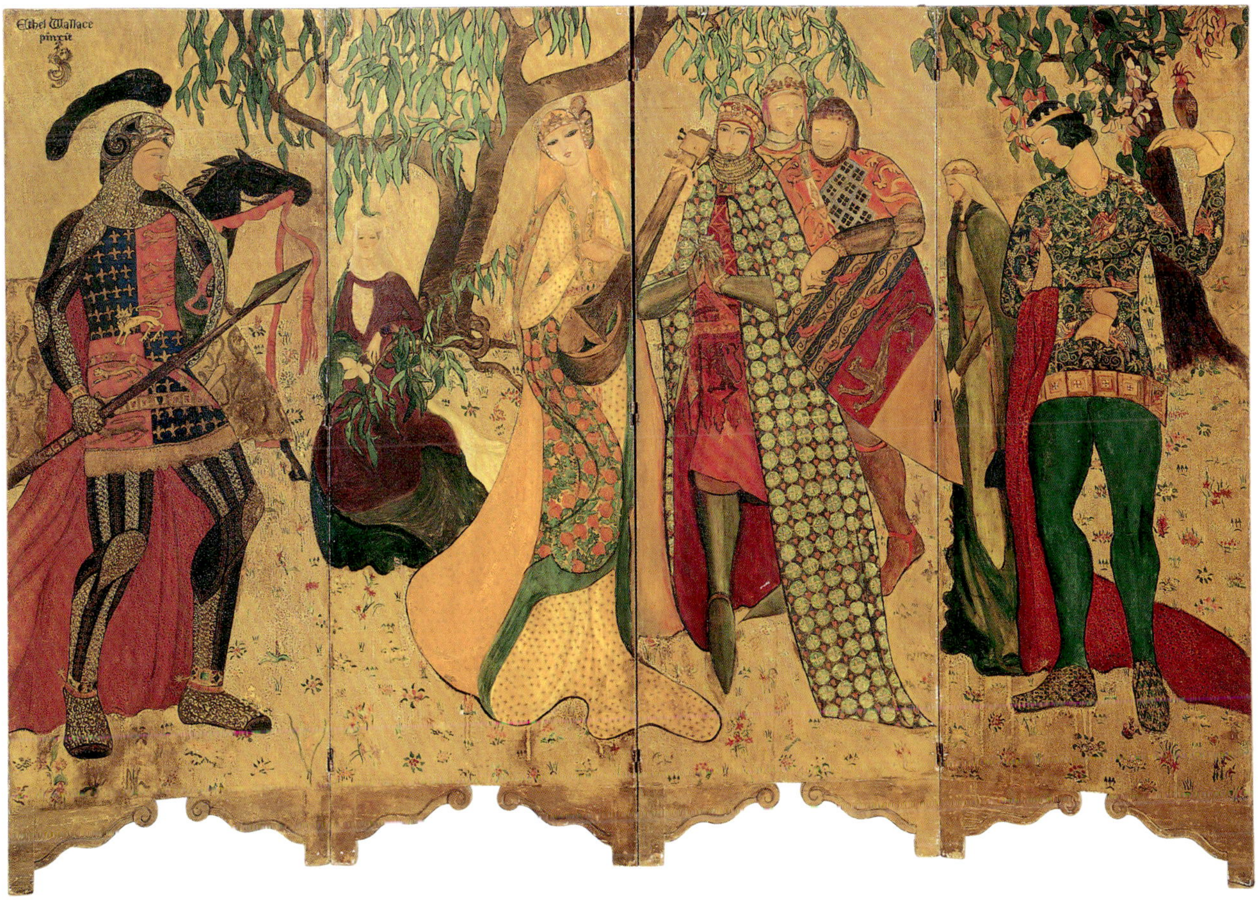

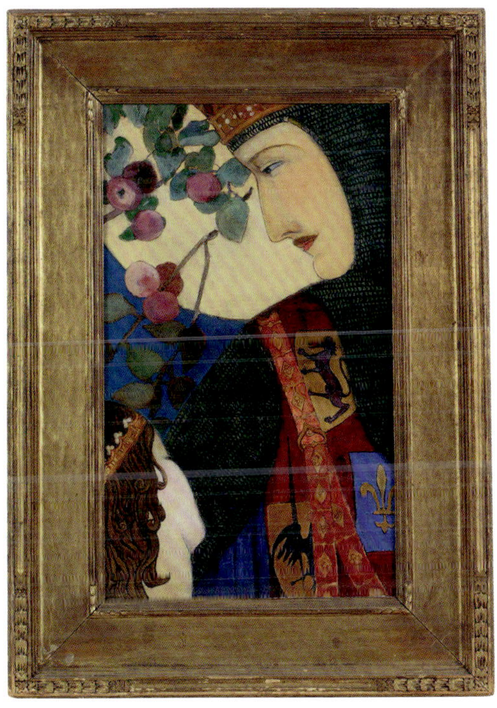

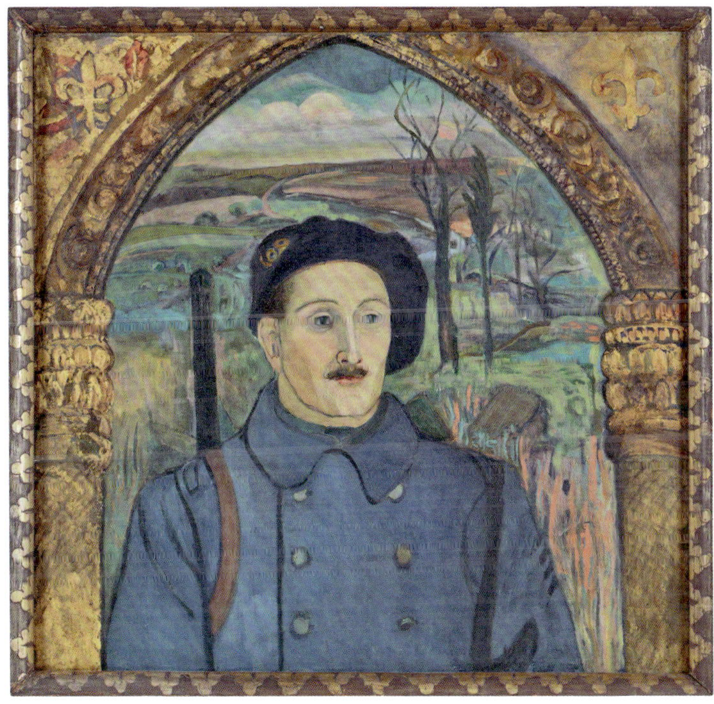

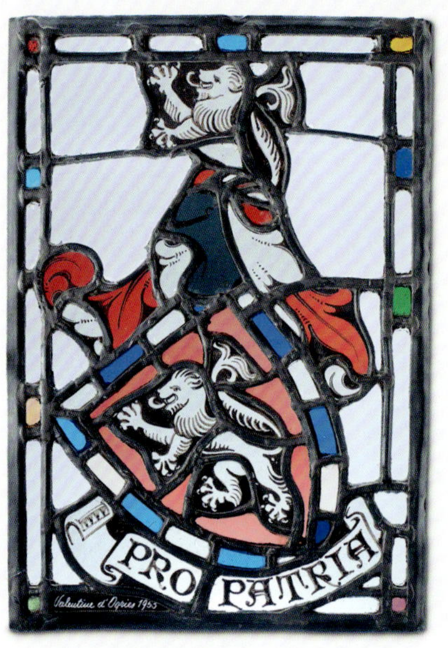

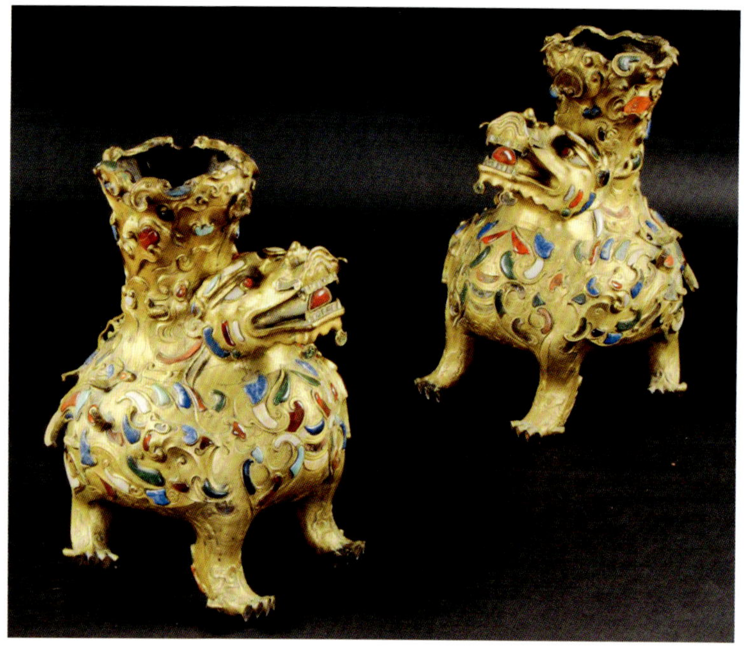

FIG. 16
Valentine D'Ogries (1889–1959), *Wallace Family Crest*, n.d. Stained glass and iron, 17⅛ × 11¼ × ¼ inches. Collection of Frederick Schillinger.

FIG. 17
Pair of Chinese jeweled gilt bronze Foo dogs, 19th century. Private collection.

FIG. 18
Ethel Wallace (1886–1968), *French Soldier (Blue Devil)* (reproduction), ca. 1918–20. Batik on silk, dimensions and location unknown. Ethel Wallace papers. Collection of the late Kristina Barbara Johnson, courtesy of Jeniah Johnson.

the United States entered the First World War, the Blue Devils marched through American cities to raise money for the war effort. It's possible that Wallace witnessed their tour through New York in 1918, when, according to local newspapers, people gathered in a three-mile-long throng to see their signature blue berets and scream, "Vive la France!"[21] Given the fervor that pervaded the city following the United States' recent, monumental decision to join the Allies, it's no wonder that Wallace was inspired to paint a portrait of a soldier so visible to the public. In one undated letter, she sheds light on the tone of that turbulent era when she writes, "Art is not produced without fierce patriotism."[22] Her portrait situates the soldier before a rolling landscape and within a gilded Gothic arch decorated with fleurs-de-lis. A batik version of *The Blue Devil* that appeared in publications throughout the 1920s makes clear that Wallace translated her oil painting into batik. Though now lost, this version visibly displays the sharper linework and flat, pared-back appearance typical of her batik portraits (Fig. 18).[23] In 1927, the batik was exhibited at the Whitney Studio Club alongside works by now-renowned artists like Mabel Dwight and Charles Sheeler, affirming her place among the moderns.[24]

Wallace's adaptation of batik was career defining. In 1917, she picked up on the medium through her fast friendship with "Javanese" folk-song performer Éva Gauthier, whom she met sometime after Gauthier's return to New York City from her travels abroad in 1914.[25] The technique requires patience and finesse; it involves sketching a design on fabric, filling in areas that should not be dyed with a wax resist, then successively dipping the fabric in baths of various colors, thereby dyeing everything except for the wax-covered areas. Wallace's use of this process can be seen in the only two known, extant iterations of a batik titled *Women around a Fountain*. We can see in the first iteration (Fig. 19) Wallace's sketch of the design, including areas where she

28

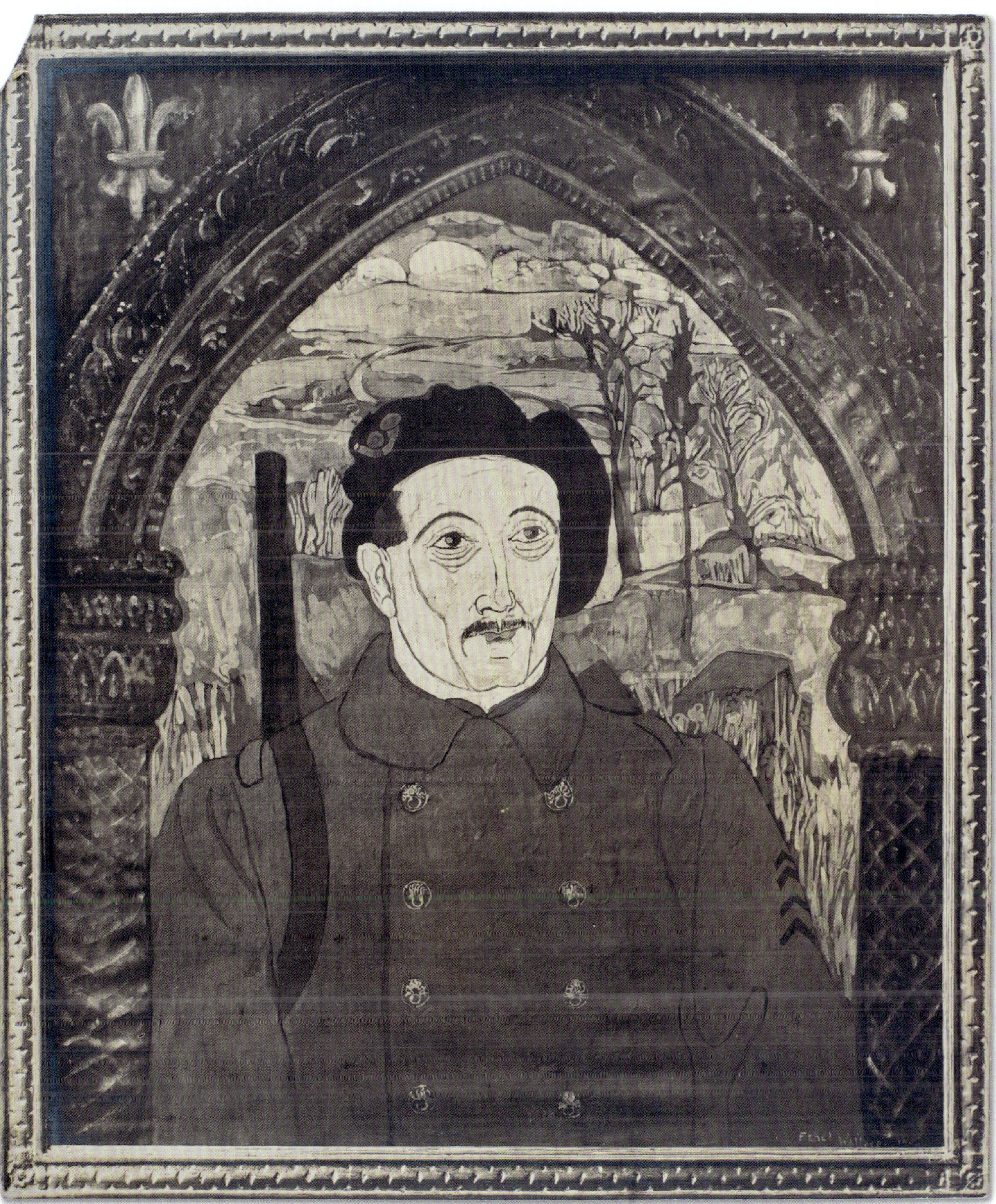

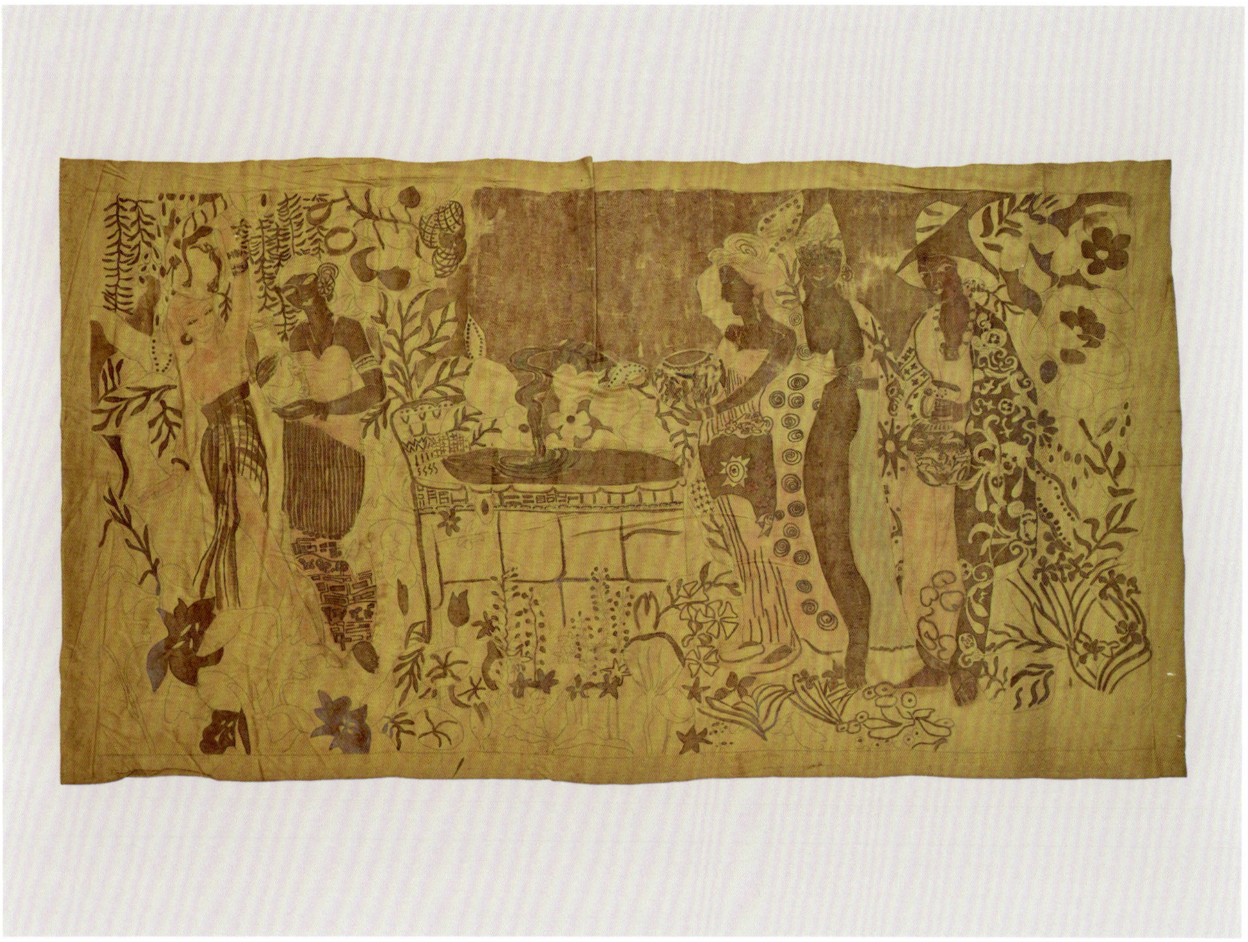

applied a brown wax. The second iteration (Fig. 20), in which the previously wax-covered areas are now bare, shows that Wallace successively dyed or hand-painted the piece with three different hues to achieve the finished (though now faded) work. The Chicago World's Columbian Exposition of 1893 introduced batik to American audiences in its Java Village. Comprising forty-six buildings, the village's display of dancers, performers, and artifacts (including batiks) impressed upon its 670,000 visitors an image of Javanese culture steeped in sensationalism and exoticism.[26] This racist presentation of living people as exotic objects for Western consumption and entertainment stemmed from American perceptions of Javanese culture as "primitive," but it nevertheless inspired interest in the culture.

With increased travel, immigration, and availability of goods from across the globe, knowledge of batik spread through publications and the work of artists who appropriated the technique.[27] Wallace, who kept her studio at 62 Washington Square, was at the heart of a group of artists working with batik in Greenwich Village, including Marguerite Zorach, a modernist who was one of the first to explore the medium.[28] Zorach picked up on the vibrant palettes and simplified forms of fauvism and cubism while in Europe between 1908 and 1911, and on her return trip to the United States, she traveled through Africa and Asia, including Indonesia, where she acquired tools for making batik.[29] Upon her

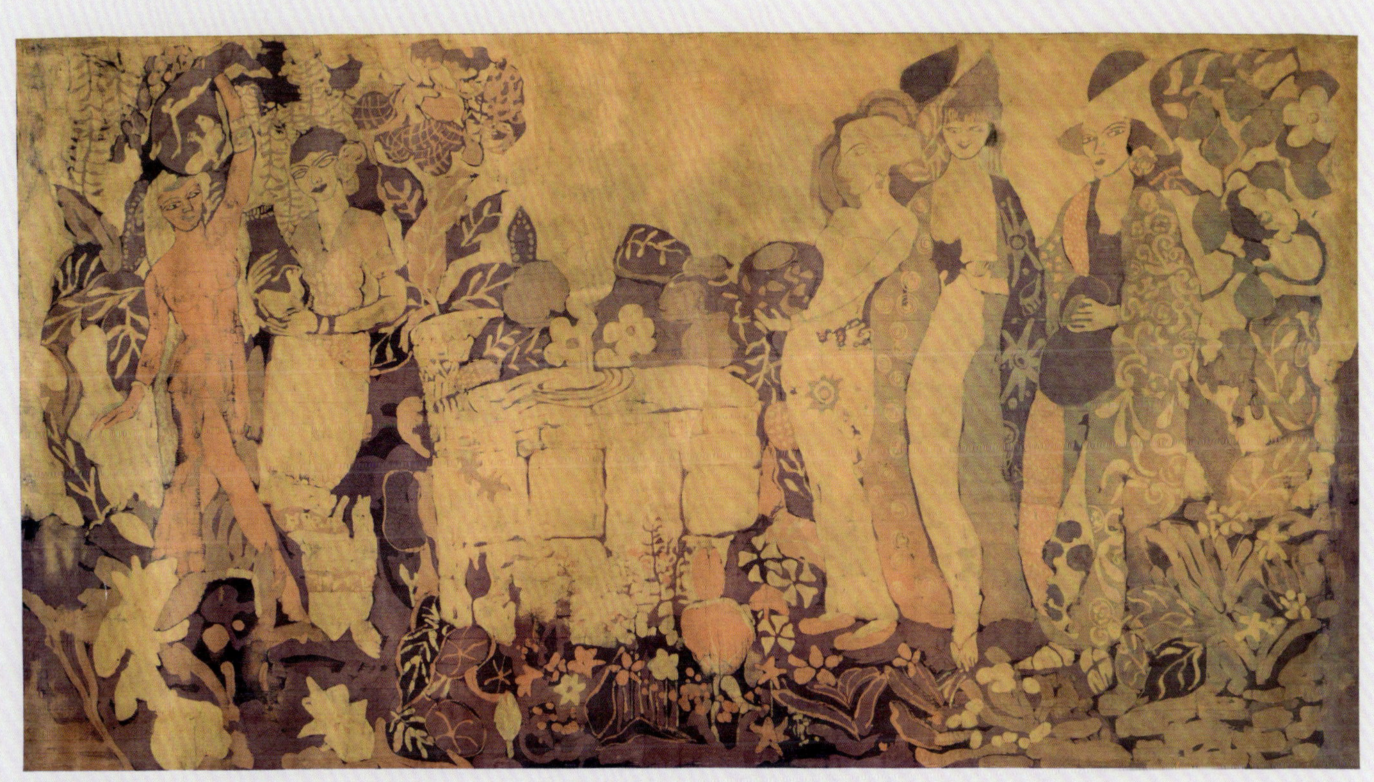

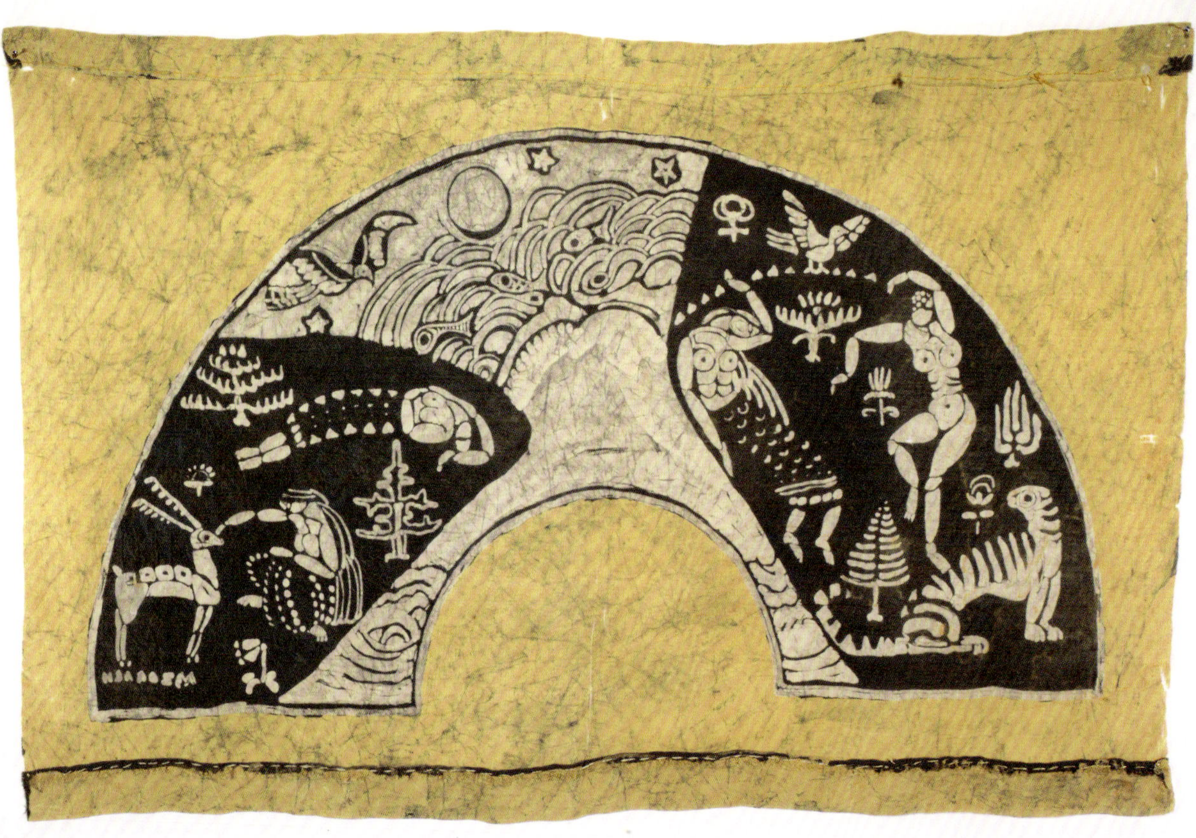

FIG. 21
Marguerite Zorach (1887–1968), *Scarf*,
n.d. Silk batik, 12⅝ × 18¾ inches. Smithsonian American Art Museum, Washington, DC, Gift from the collection of
Tessim Zorach, 1968.87.1.

return, she produced clothing and bedding featuring stylized nude figures and animals (Fig. 21).[30] Wallace never traveled to Indonesia herself,
but became enamored with batik once it made its way to the United
States. In a letter to a collector of her work, she wrote:

> When batik made its first appearance in this country—it
> was a craft. People made ornamental patterns very much
> in the style of the Javanese themselves. It came to my
> attention—I tried painting one day in that warmer just to
> see what it was like. It was so fascinating that I kept on and
> realized that here was a medium for the modern artist to
> paint on beautiful fabrics.[31]

As a medium that can be traced to cultures as early as first-century
Egypt, batik does not immediately strike one as modern. Fashion historian Abby Lillethun draws parallels between batik and modernism by
pointing out the latter movement's ties to folk art and "primitive" art
forms, most famously recognized in the influence of traditional Afri-
can masks on Pablo Picasso's artwork.[32] More specifically, she writes,
"Javanese batik's flat design, clearly delineated line, abstracted natural forms, and emphasis on rhythm coincide with the conventional-
ized formal elements of Art Nouveau."[33] Wallace's appropriation of the
medium allowed her to achieve a unique, modern aesthetic redolent of

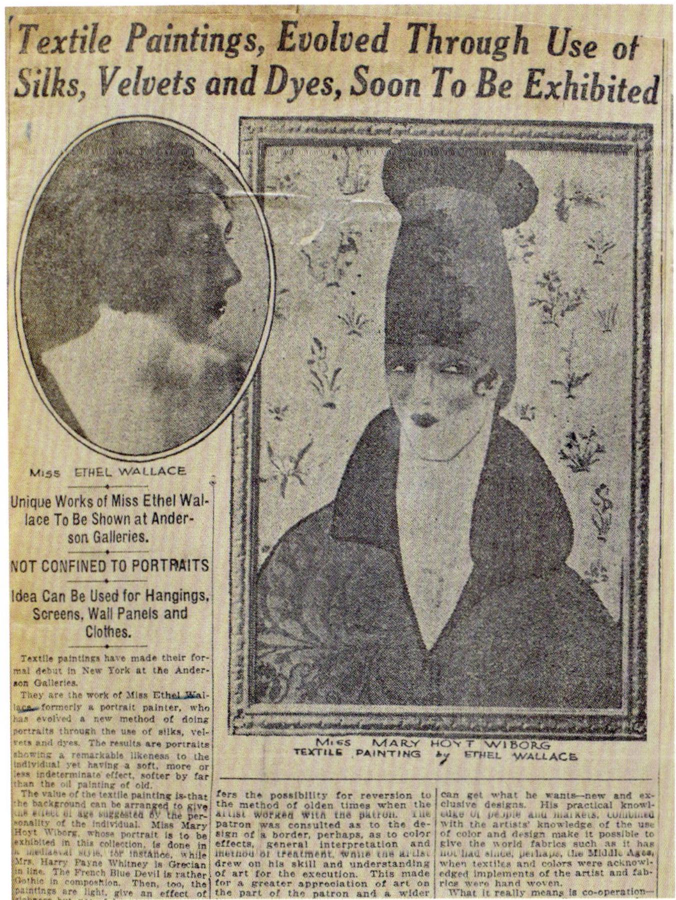

Textile Paintings, Evolved Through Use of Silks, Velvets and Dyes, Soon To Be Exhibited

MISS ETHEL WALLACE

Unique Works of Miss Ethel Wallace To Be Shown at Anderson Galleries.

NOT CONFINED TO PORTRAITS

Idea Can Be Used for Hangings, Screens, Wall Panels and Clothes.

Textile paintings have made their formal debut in New York at the Anderson Galleries.

They are the work of Miss Ethel Wallace, formerly a portrait painter, who has evolved a new method of doing portraits through the use of silks, velvets and dyes. The results are portraits showing a remarkable likeness to the individual yet having a soft, more or less indeterminate effect, softer by far than the oil painting of old.

The value of the textile painting is that the background can be arranged to give the effect of age suggested by the personality of the individual. Miss Mary Hoyt Wiborg, whose portrait is to be exhibited in this collection, is done in a mediaeval style, for instance, while Mrs. Harry Payne Whitney is Grecian in line. The French Blue Devil is rather Gothic in composition. Then, too, the paintings are light, give an effect of [...] fers the possibility for reversion to the method of olden times when the artist worked with the patron. The patron was consulted as to the design of a border, perhaps, as to color effects, general interpretation and method of treatment, while the artist drew on his skill and understanding of art for the execution. This made for a greater appreciation of art on the part of the patron and a wider can get what he wants—new and exclusive designs. His practical knowledge of people and markets, combined with the artists' knowledge of the use of color and design make it possible to give the world fabrics such as it has not had since, perhaps, the Middle Ages, when textiles and colors were acknowledged implements of the artist and fabrics were hand woven.

What it really means is co-operation—

MISS MARY HOYT WIBORG
TEXTILE PAINTING by ETHEL WALLACE

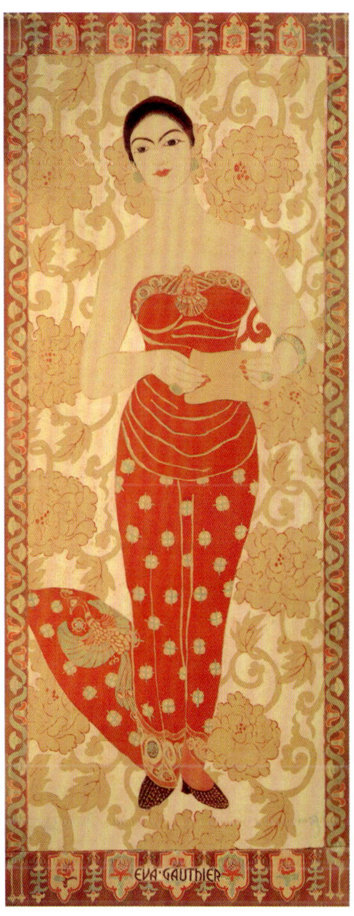

worldliness and luxury that became trendy among New York's elite, and she began to make portraits of society women in batik.[34]

Her batik portraits and fashion designs swept through the city, compelling her to work part-time in Bucks County, where she had more space for her various vats of dyes. Back in New York, journalists toured her studio for feature articles that served as free advertising, as seen in this excerpt from the *Daily Garment News*:

> Included in the collection at her studio (much of her work is being exhibited at art galleries) is a strip of three and one-half yards of sapphire blue velvet, upon which is the batik of an oval pale geranium rose design. The piece is priced at $200. It is suggested as particularly suitable for an evening cape.[35]

In today's money, this yardage was offered at $3,000. Her portraits, on the other hand, sold for today's equivalent of $45,000. Prized among Wallace's batik portraits were her highly publicized depictions of Mary Hoyt Wiborg and Éva Gauthier (Figs. 22 and 23). Standing at seven feet tall, Gauthier's portrait is a life-sized, stylized portrayal of the petite, four-foot-eleven singer, whose chic figure floats dreamily against a floral backdrop, a sheet of music clutched between her delicate fingers. Between Gauthier's gown, her accessories, and the swirling floral patterns, the portrait encapsulates the glitzy, extravagant era in which it was made and showcases Wallace's skill in achieving precise linework and color in a medium that was new to her.[36]

Equally well received as her portraits were her batik "paintings" and feminist interpretations of biblical figures like Eve and Salome (Fig. 24). Her only extant velvet painting (for which she still used the batik method of dyeing), though now significantly faded, recalls her earlier, impressionistic aesthetic, while her portraits of women remain cleaner in linework (Fig. 25). Once again formulated from an amalgamation of different cultural styles, Wallace's Eve stands on Egyptian-style feet before one of art nouveau's favorite motifs, the peacock; her single exposed breast evokes ancient Minoan and Khmer approaches to the female figure (Fig. 26). As a woman who took what she wanted despite a literal command from God, Eve is one of the most notorious rebels of all time. Despite the story's moralizing lesson about original sin, which has been used for millennia to malign and suppress women, Wallace's Eve does not appear fearful or regretful, as she does in other art histori-cal works, but stares straight back at us, with the symbol of sin wrapped around her neck and the infamous apple displayed cheekily within her grip. With her attitude and references to West Asian and South Asian styles, Wallace links her Eve to Eden's projected real-world location near Mesopotamia and the Persian Gulf, thereby rejecting the passive and remorseful European Eve and replacing her with an empowered and unapologetic goddess of Mesopotamia.

With equal zeal, Wallace's Salome dances euphorically before the cast-aside severed head of John the Baptist, whose death she demanded following his condemnation of her divorced mother's new marriage (Fig. 27). In her book *Female Spectacle*, Susan Glenn writes that the idea of the New Woman found expression in Eastern cultures whose sensual dances allowed women a freedom of sexuality deemed radical in the United States.[37] Salome received the head of John the Baptist because her stepfather, Herod Antipas, was impressed by her dancing. Glenn writes, "[Dancing] was radical too because the right to be sexually expressive along with the right to work and to vote was an off-stage polit-ical issue for younger women who, after 1910, would identify themselves as feminists."[38] In the early twentieth century, sexually assertive interpre-tations of Salome's dance on the vaudeville stage inspired a public obses-sion dubbed "Salomania."[39] One critic wrote, "She is bad, and that is a great element in her attraction."[40] The Salome trend appealed to the rebel in Ethel, who was herself the sexually open epitome of the New Woman. In a multipage feature of Wallace's work published in the arts magazine *International Studio*, the author commends the artist on her interpreta-tion in batik:

> One feels that for once a woman has interpreted a woman,
> who, like Cleopatra and Lucretia Borgia, has been too often
> painted by men, and doubtless misjudged; not so much
> cruel as indifferent, not so much blood-lustful as simply

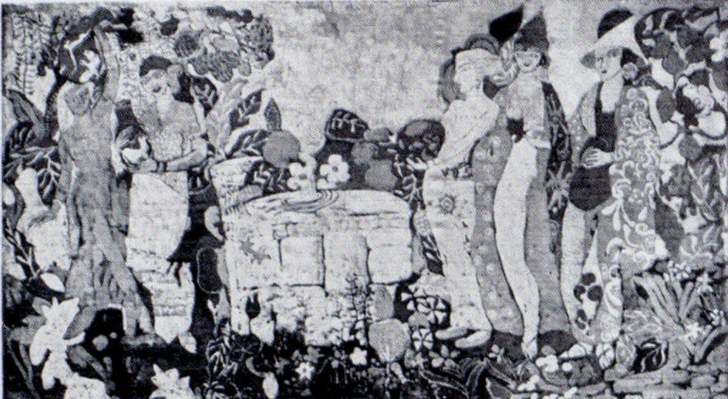

"WOMEN AROUND A FOUNTAIN" BY ETHEL WALLACE

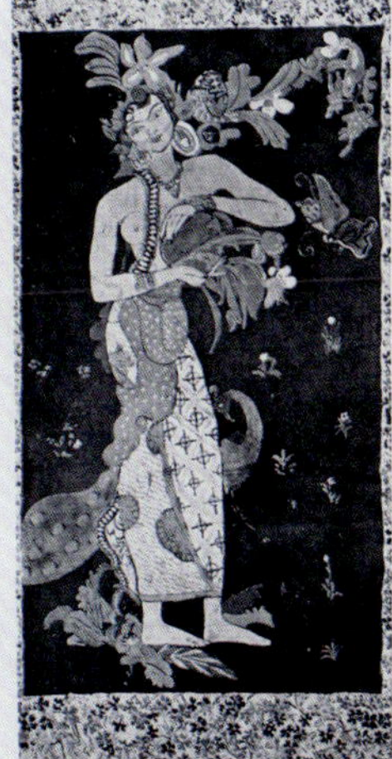

out and replaced with a fresh coating of hot wax, and each tone or touch of color achieved by dippings in a carefully compounded dye-color. She says of her work in batik: "It is an experiment to see how far one may go with a medium that has had little honor done to it."

This is the craft side, which, as a framework, supports the opulent fantasy of this artist's fullness of life. She believes that the artist should be the consummate craftsman, able to regard the chosen substances as means to an end, as millstones to render wheat and red poppies into fine flour for the feast of beauty. She tells us a legend of Persia, or Cambodia, or Ionia, and conveys to us the repose of profane goddesses who were more sacred than the others, who knew no wrong, who had no nerves, but an abundant and beautiful serenity and a sure grace more profound than sadness. Ethel Wallace uses her fantasy not as mere decoration, but as a colorful and sufficing commentary and precipitate of life. One says at first glance "Persian," and then, "No—but as Persia might have produced had Persia had the life of today in her alembic."

Of the batiks reproduced here, "Eve and the Peacock" is done with an easy and un-neurotic sensuousness. The work is a life-scale panel, a cool and complex harmony of yellow-green flesh tone, as fresh as half-ripened apples, with a sanguine butterfly and a pomegranate and a rich border of red, black and yellow. "Women Around the Fountain," done on pale silk in

"EVE AND THE PEACOCK" BY ETHEL WALLACE

nacre-blue and crushed violet and remote rose color and saffron, is a ballad of the feelings of womankind—a gamut of five figures, like the five notes of a Grecian scale, dissonant to each other, women of varying demeanor, or perhaps five transmutations of one woman: the materialist who seeks water for culinary use, the maker of wine, the idle and apathetic hedonist who cares only for the song of the fountain, the dancer whose water-jar is only a symbol, the weary figure who seeks peace at a primitive source. The portrait called "Nouripanûr," in warm violets, wine-colors, bluish lavenders, with cold blue ideographic flowers on a Chinese white ground, is a Persian reading of a modern woman's face and personality. The configuration is bold and simple, done with a free gesture and a fantastic yet definite sense of *décor*. "Salomé" is in the pose of Shiva, a poised movement in pale green and terra cotta and flat Chinese yellow, with flesh the color of dried citron. The head of John the

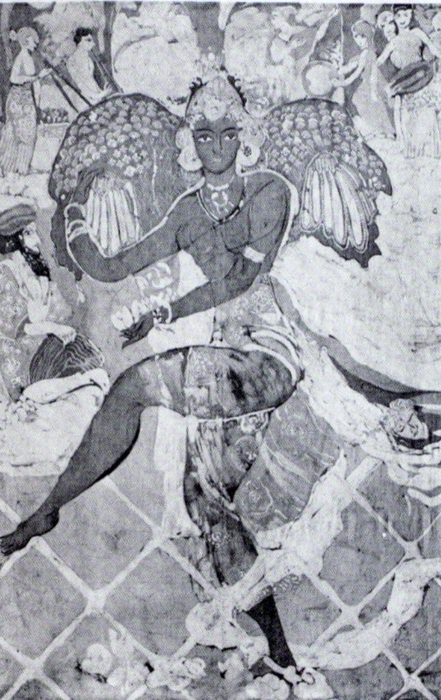

"SALOMÉ" BATIK BY ETHEL WALLACE

Baptist is only a minor detail, in a corner, unimportant as compared with the sinuous and voluptuous dancer. Here is a Salomé who, having gained her whim, is no longer interested in the head, but gives herself to dancing. She might be Shiva, celebrating the full impulse of the moment. She recalls the spirited and abandoned mural sculptures of the palaces of Cambodia, and the untrammelled jubilation of the Ajanta frescoes, done in an age before sin was thought of; voluptuous and unashamed in line and motion and addressed to the finer sensuousness of the mind. A living figure dances, with a background of legendary things, replete with suggestion and imagery, depicting rather the half-indicated shadowy race-relics one perceives in a living woman than the marionettes that surround the story of Salomé. One feels that for once a woman has interpreted a woman, who, like Cleopatra and Lucretia Borgia, has been too often painted by men, and doubtless misjudged; not so much cruel as indifferent, not so much blood-lustful as simply sensuous; in a word: a woman has dared to be herself, regardless of her time and environment, and has visualized the unchanging spirit of this type of womanhood. The result is a Twentieth Century expression of an ageless truth.

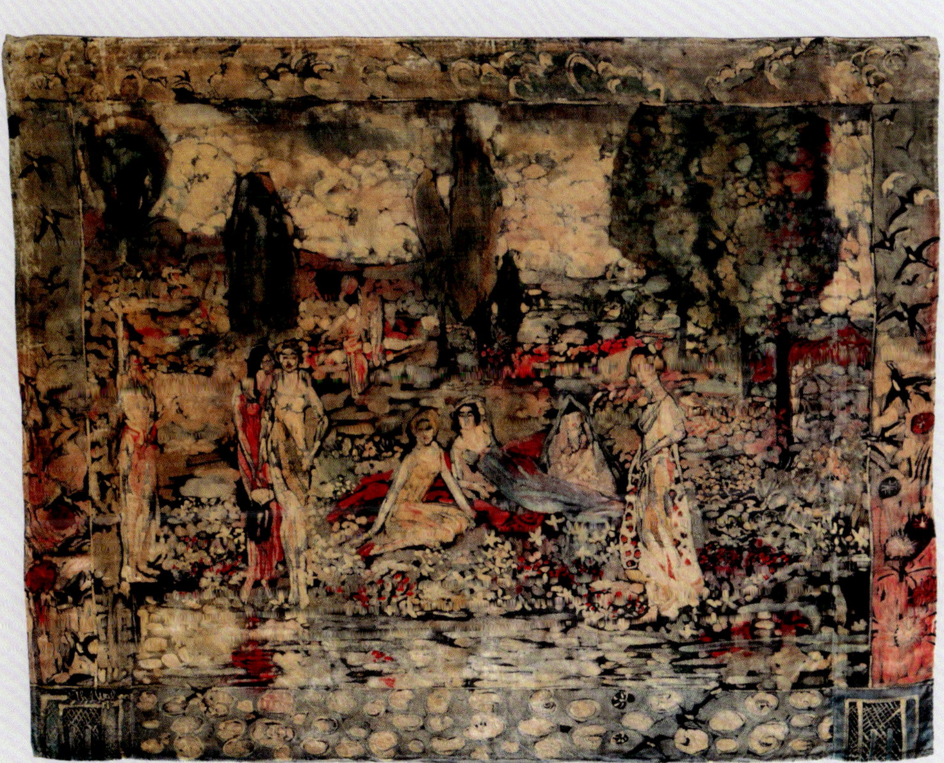

FIG. 26
Ethel Wallace (1886–1968), *Eve and the Peacock*, ca. 1919. Silkscreen scroll, 75 × 37 inches. Collection of the late Kristina Barbara Johnson, courtesy of Jeniah Johnson.

FIG. 27
Ethel Wallace (1886–1968), *Salome*, ca. 1919. Silkscreen scroll, 83 × 42½ inches. Collection of the late Kristina Barbara Johnson, courtesy of Jeniah Johnson.

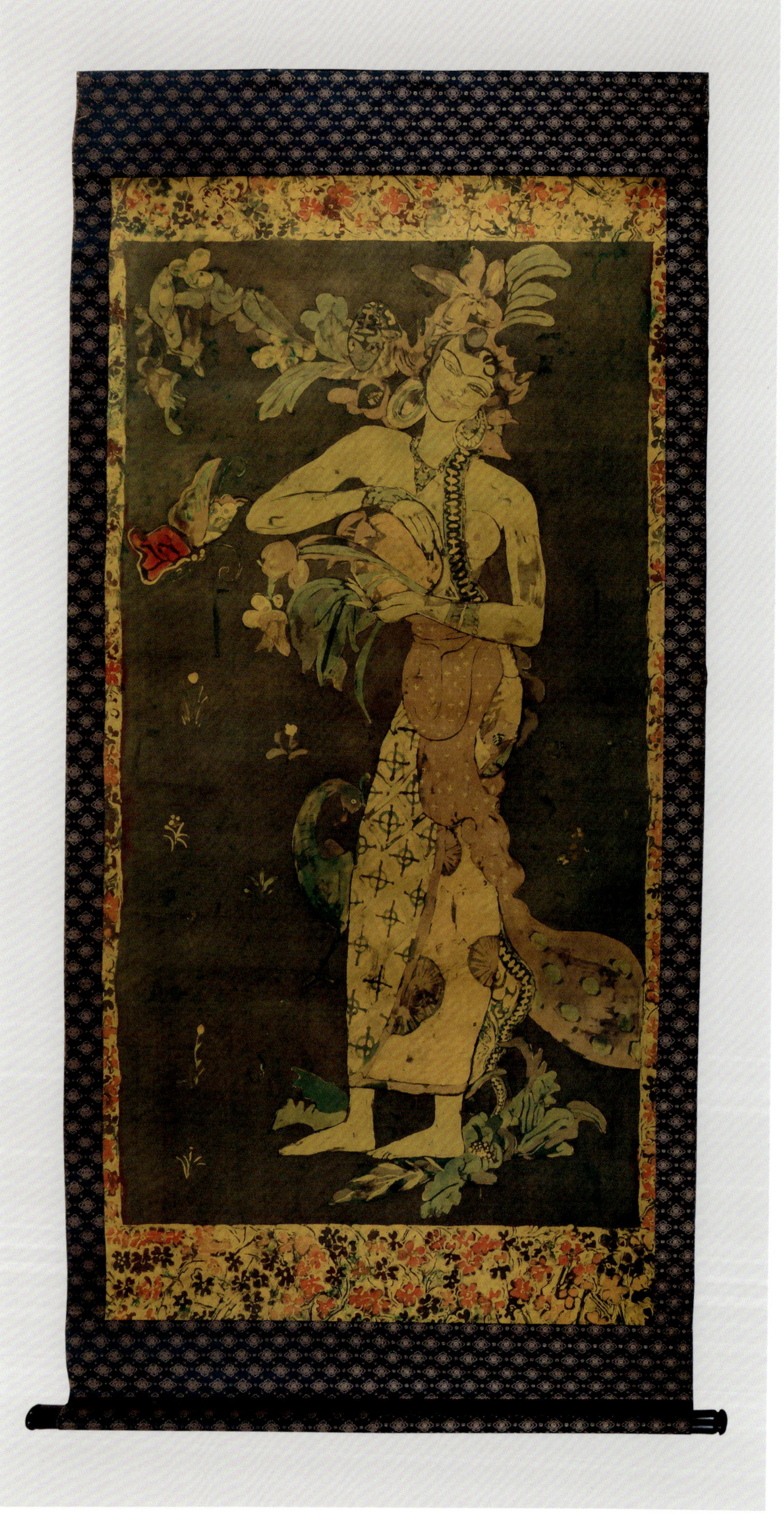

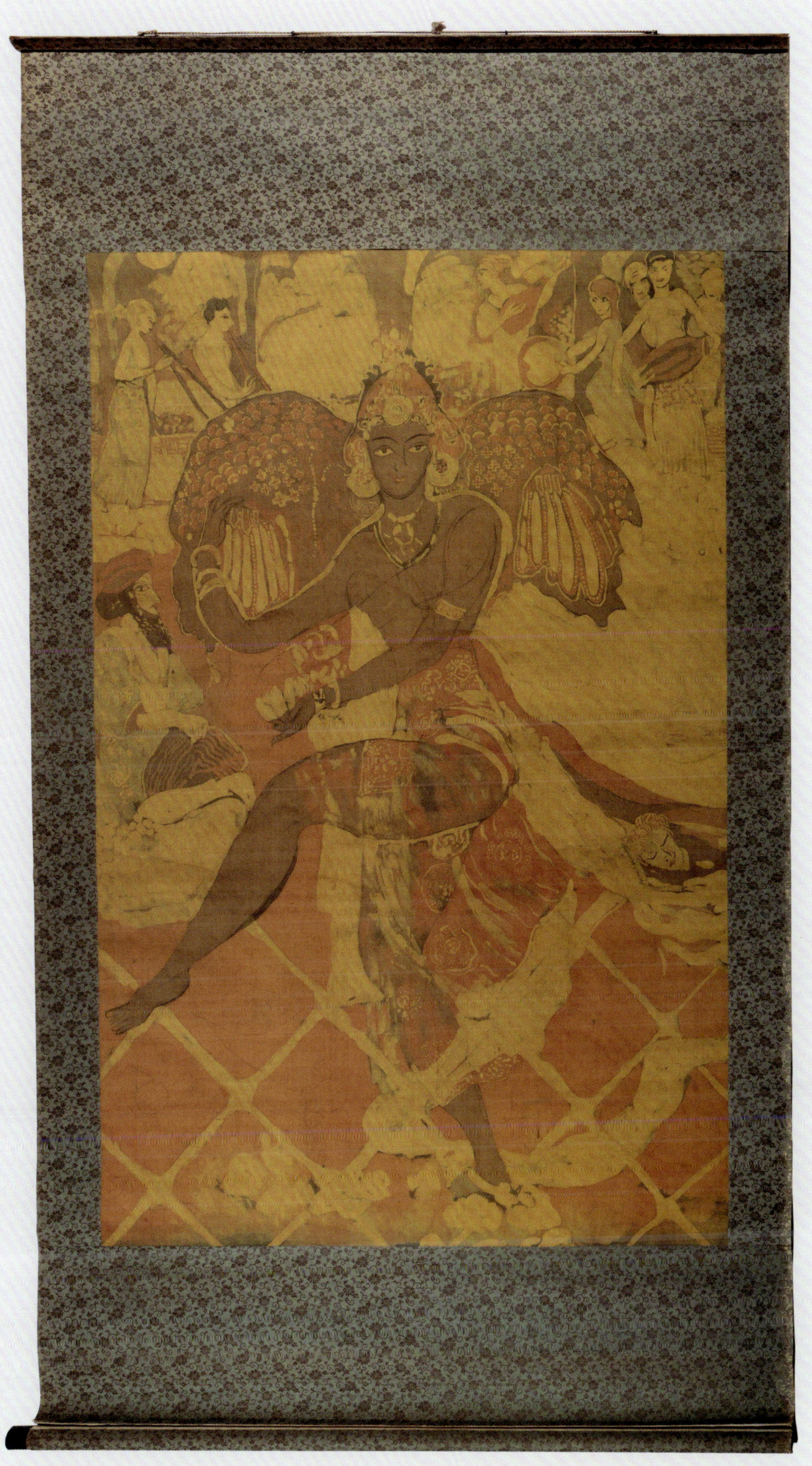

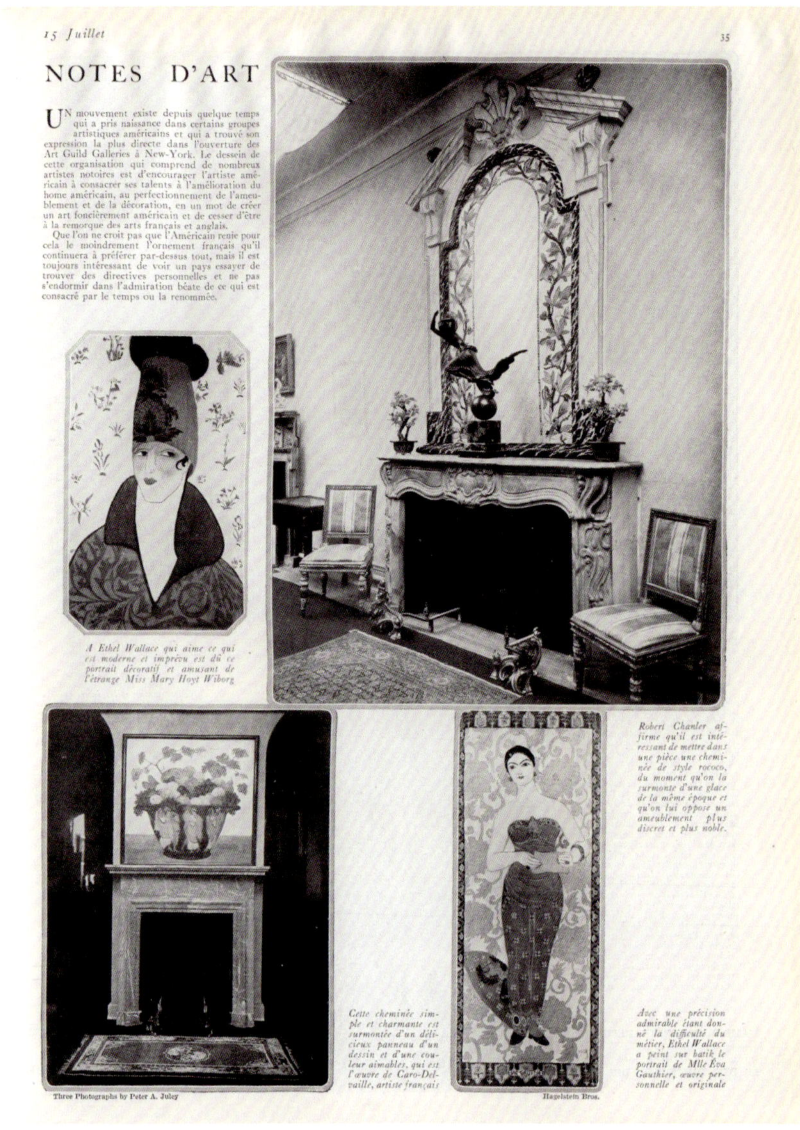

sensuous; in a word: a woman has dared to be herself, regardless of her time and environment, and has visualized the unchanging spirit of this type of womanhood. The result is a Twentieth Century expression of ageless truth.[41]

In a technical sense, Wallace's batiks were praised for their beautiful compositions, vibrant color, and sheen. In a particularly enthusiastic review, one critic wrote:

> Her velvets and silks seem to glow with passion, shimmer with moonbeams or sing with the songs of the fairy forests in a manner which has not been possible to oil paint on canvas. She veritably poetizes in color, vibrates in color, and her work is always personal, fanciful and free from either hackneyed tradition or tiresome affectation.[42]

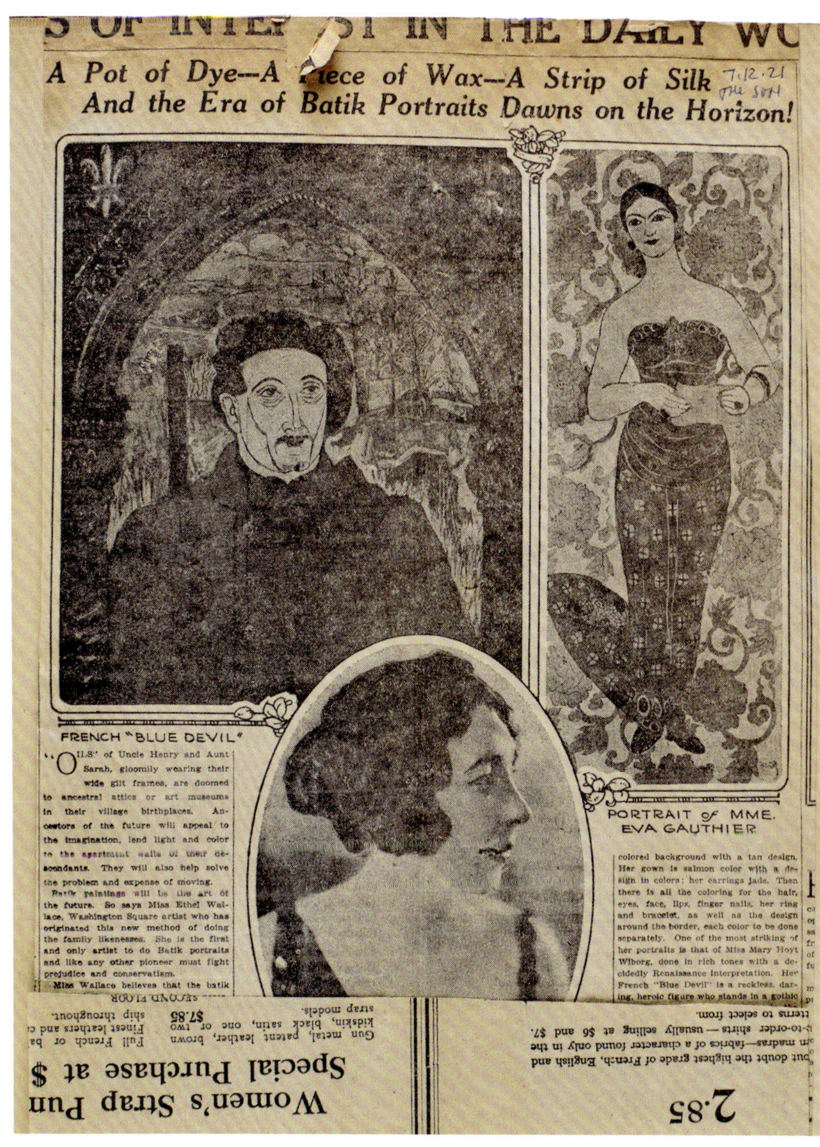

By 1921, the press declared Wallace a pioneer in batik portraits, the "newest rage in art," and *Vogue Paris* described the portraits as "personal and original" and "modern and unexpected" in its July issue.[43] Splashed across publications were her face, her work, and announcements of exhibitions held throughout the United States, London, and Paris (Figs. 28 and 29). Gertrude Whitney held an exhibition of Wallace's work at her New York studio, and Wallace traveled to Paris to pitch her designs to the couturiers.[44] In London, one journalist's description had Wallace dipping entire rooms in dyes, then standing triumphantly among her designs as buyers arrived (Fig. 30):

> They call Miss Ethel Wallace the Batik girl in New York, because she has dressed smart New York women and their rooms in Batik. The other day she had transformed one room of the Leicester Galleries into a mystery of silks and velvets and crepes wrought with wonderful colours and beautiful designs, and she stood in the midst of it all in a

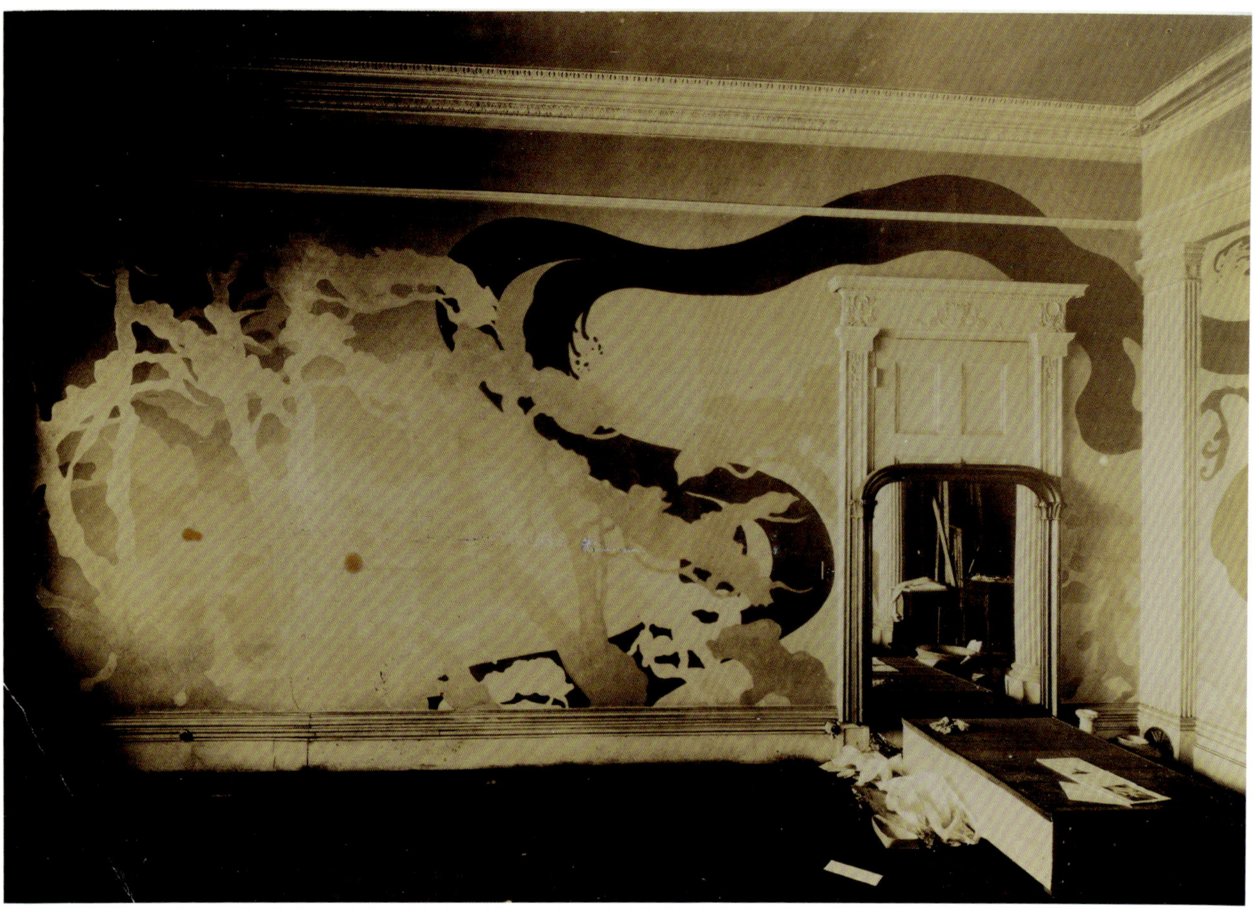

Batik frock of canary-yellow accordion-pleated skirt and a smock of cloth of silver shimmering with yellow, pink, blue, and mauve. There were decorative panels and Batik portraits and yards of material designed for furniture and more yards for frocks, and any number of those mysterious folk who are hidden in the recesses of smart dressmakers' establishments designing came to decide whether to Batik or not to Batik our autumn gowns. . . . If you take proper interest in Batik Miss Wallace will show you what Mrs. Harry Payne Whitney and other smart women wear as Batik teagowns in their Batik rooms.[45]

Her success propelled her to open her own shop in Midtown Manhattan, across the street from what is now Rockefeller Center. She designed custom clothing and was commissioned by luxury retailers like Hickson, Bonwit Teller, and Robert McBratney & Co. to produce hand-printed linens and thousands of yards of dyed velvet and crepe (Figs. 31–33).[46]

Like her batik portraits, her fashion designs were self-taught and intended to send a message. With the invention of bloomers, loose-fitting knee-length trousers worn by women underneath their dresses, in the 1850s, women's fashion in the United States had already turned to Eastern cultures for inspiration.[47] Bloomers signified a challenge to gender norms and were thus associated with radical feminist politics, resulting in

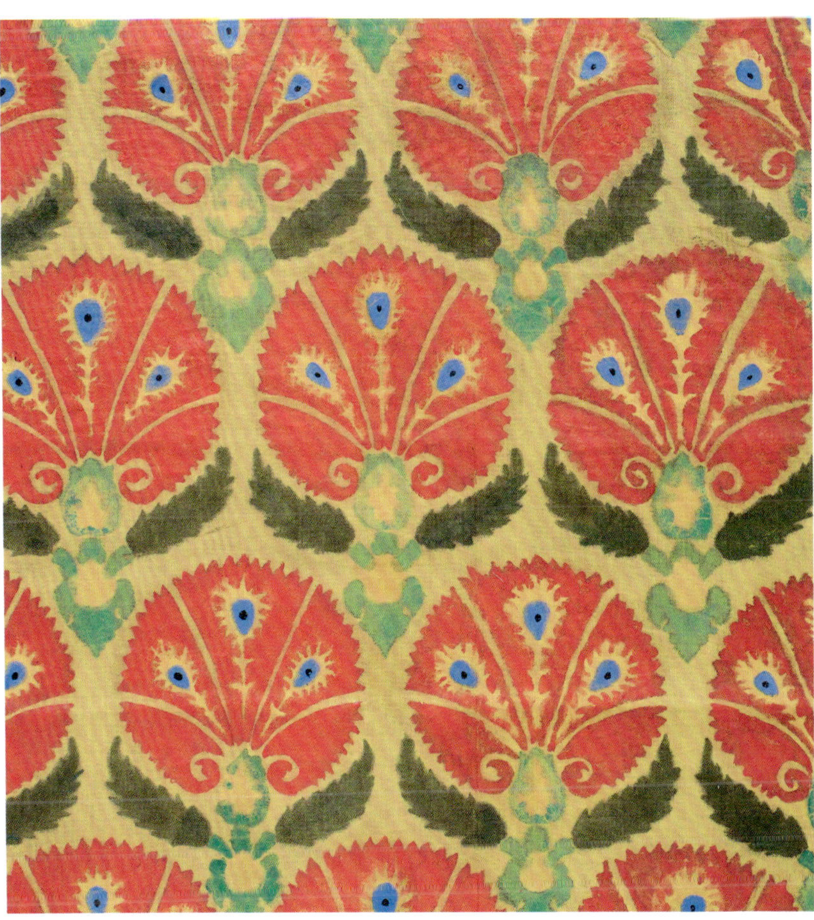

FIG. 31
Sample of a printed fabric by Wallace.
Collection of the late Kristina Barbara
Johnson, courtesy of Jeniah Johnson.

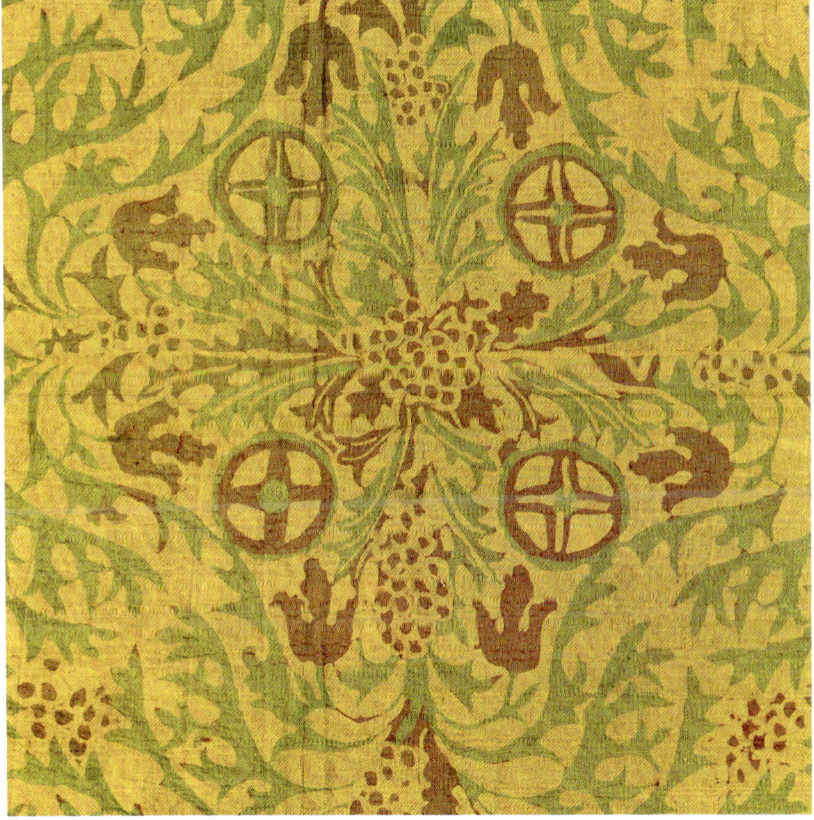

FIG. 32
Sample of a printed fabric by Wallace.
Collection of the late Kristina Barbara
Johnson, courtesy of Jeniah Johnson.

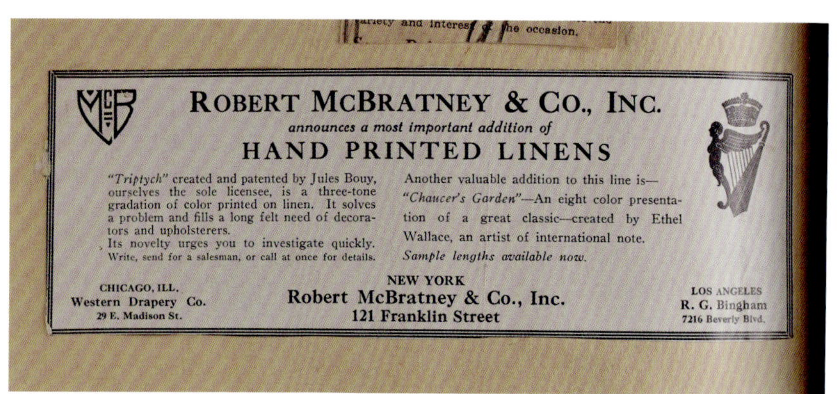

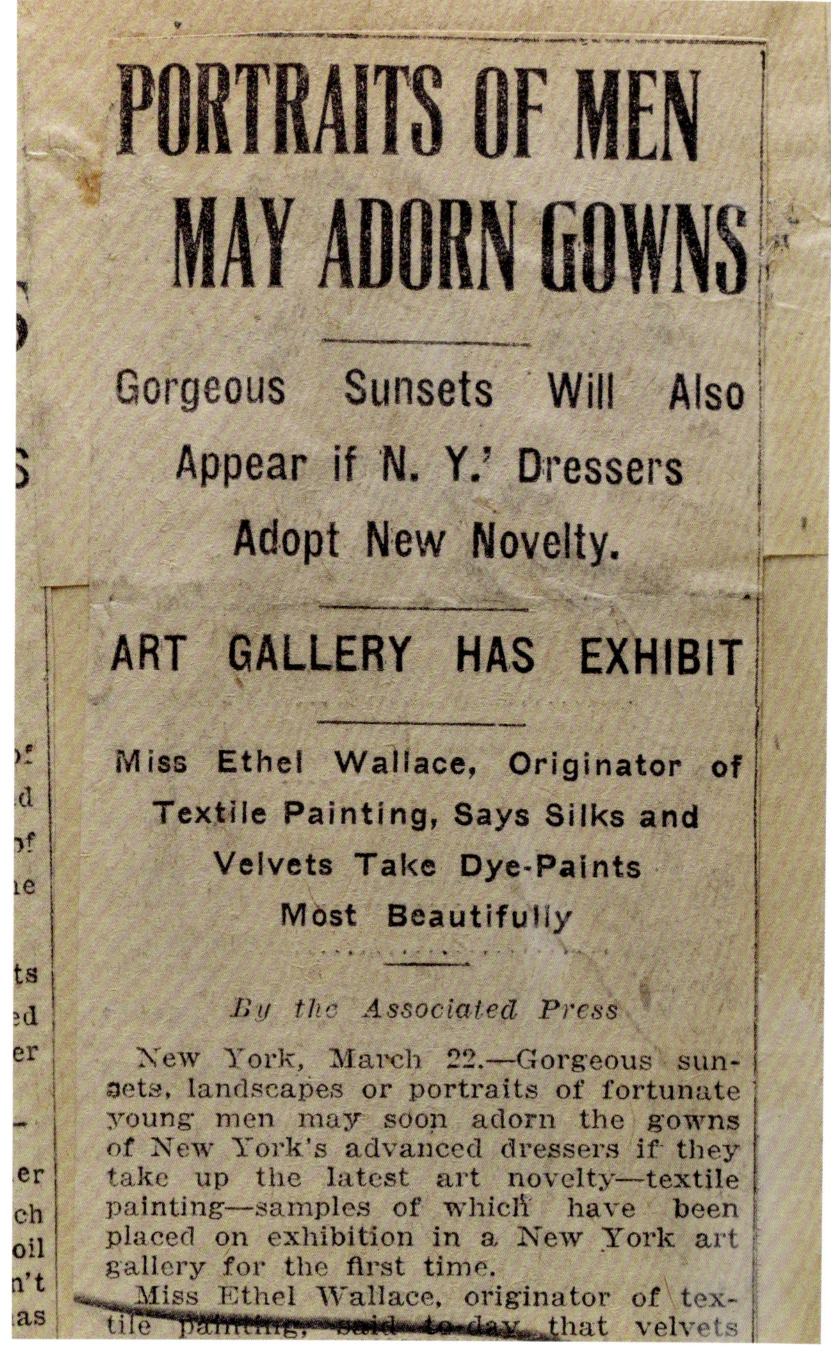

FIG. 34
Newspaper clipping from Wallace's scrapbook. Ethel Wallace papers. Collection of the late Kristina Barbara Johnson, courtesy of Jeniah Johnson.

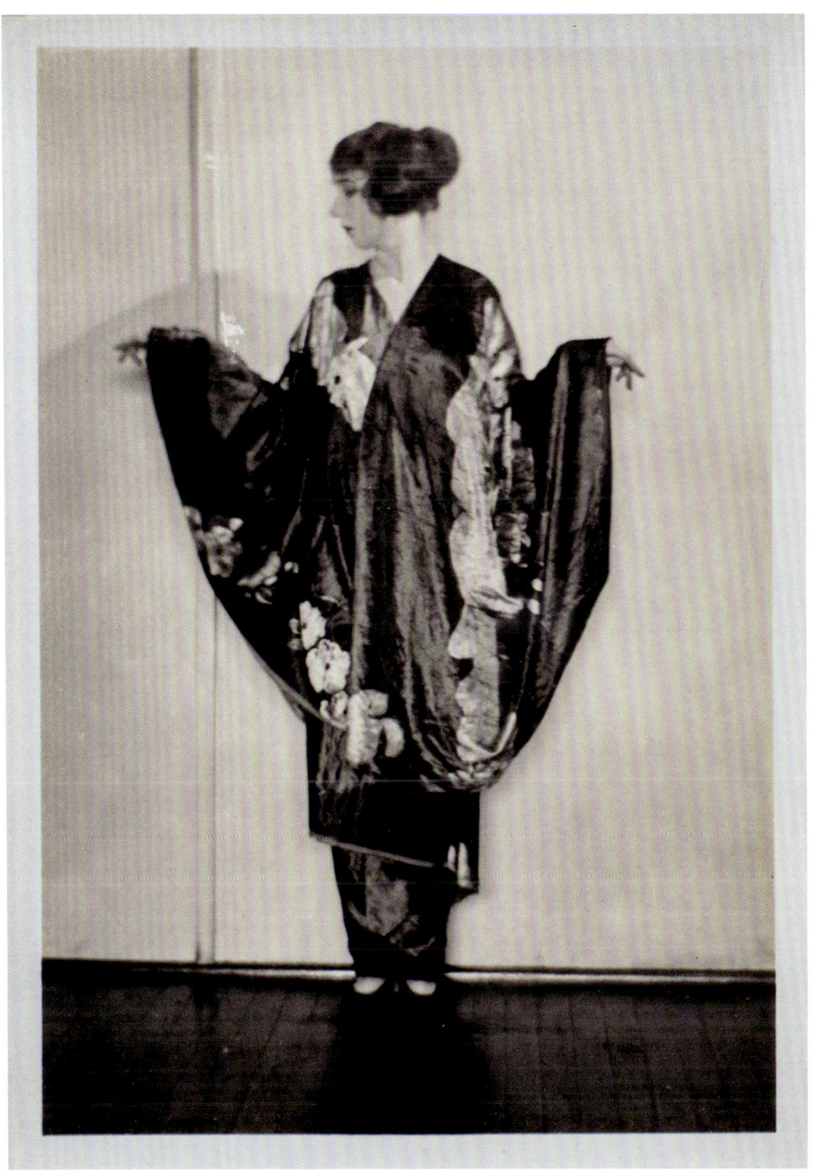

the trend's failure to gain widespread popularity in that earlier era.[48] In the 1920s, women's fashion again adapted aspects of Eastern dress to create a style more relaxed and comfortable than the Victorian era's form-fitting S silhouette.[49] The new straighter, looser dress silhouettes allowed for a more sensual idea of women's bodies that corresponded to women's freedom and the idea of the New Woman.[50] As Michael Mamp argues in his essay in this catalogue, Wallace may have also been influenced by the Eastern-inspired creations of the French designer Paul Poiret. Her designs reflected progressive fashion ideas aligned with the New Woman, and even dared to approach gender-bending intentions when she painted the faces of men on flowing gowns (Fig. 34).[51] According to lore, she famously painted her lovers' faces on one of her own coats, then wore it around town. Loose in silhouette and made to order, her clothing was cut to fall with the same ease as her mellifluous lines on paper and silk; in one photo, she models a robe with arms outstretched, velvet hanging like wings (Fig. 35).

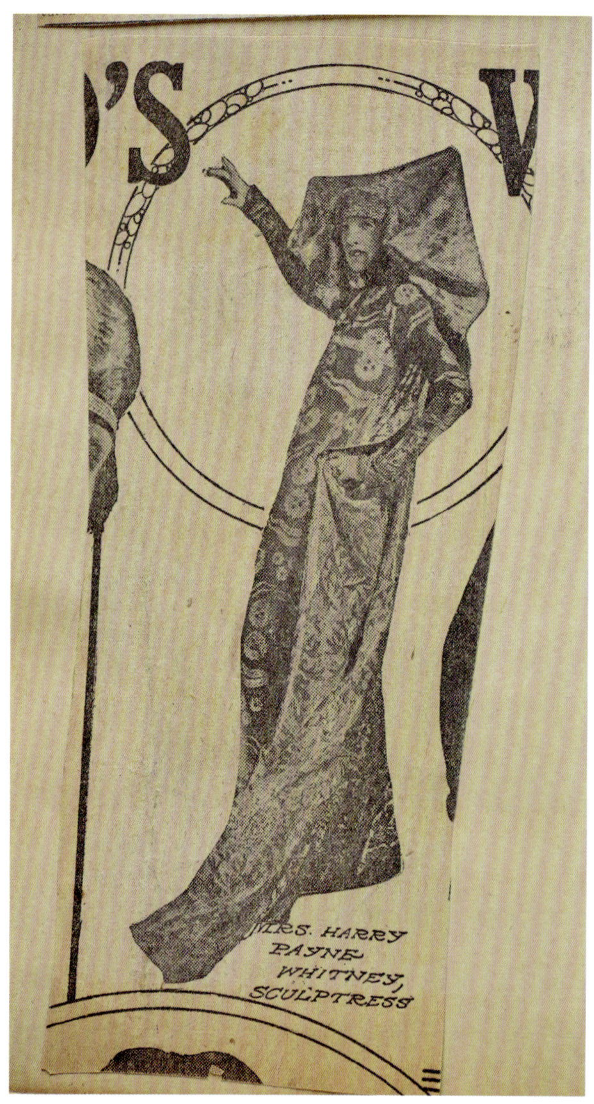

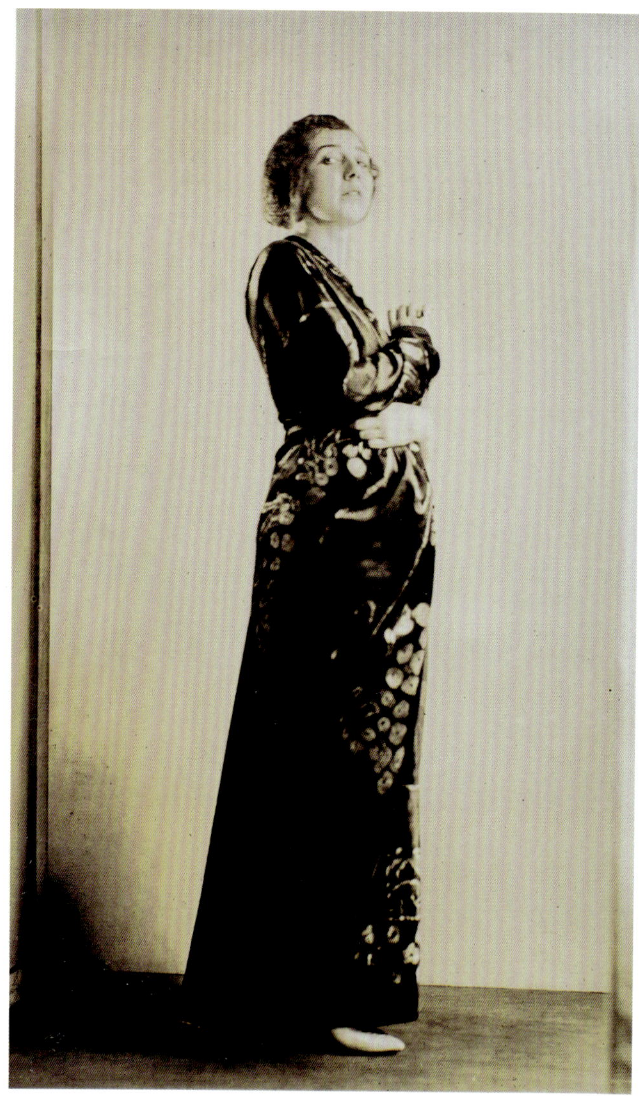

For her clients, her designs served as unique, collectable garments through which to express their individuality and commitment to
the avant-garde and countercultures. They were met with enthusiasm by
figures like Whitney, whose photograph in which she wears a garment
by Wallace was distributed to New York newspapers (Fig. 36).[52] Photographs of the artist modeling her own clothing show her as defiant and
imposing, and capture the personality people still speak of today (Figs. 37
and 38). With her portraits and her designs, Wallace elevated the independent women she held in high regard—including herself—and dressed
them in clothing designed to give them the confidence and freedom to be
who they wanted to be.

PRAYER TO THE GREAT CAT

At some point during the New York years, the door of Wallace's Washington Square studio was opened by Rafael Abreu, a dashing Spanish count
whose impact on her life and work would be resounding (Figs. 39–41).[53]

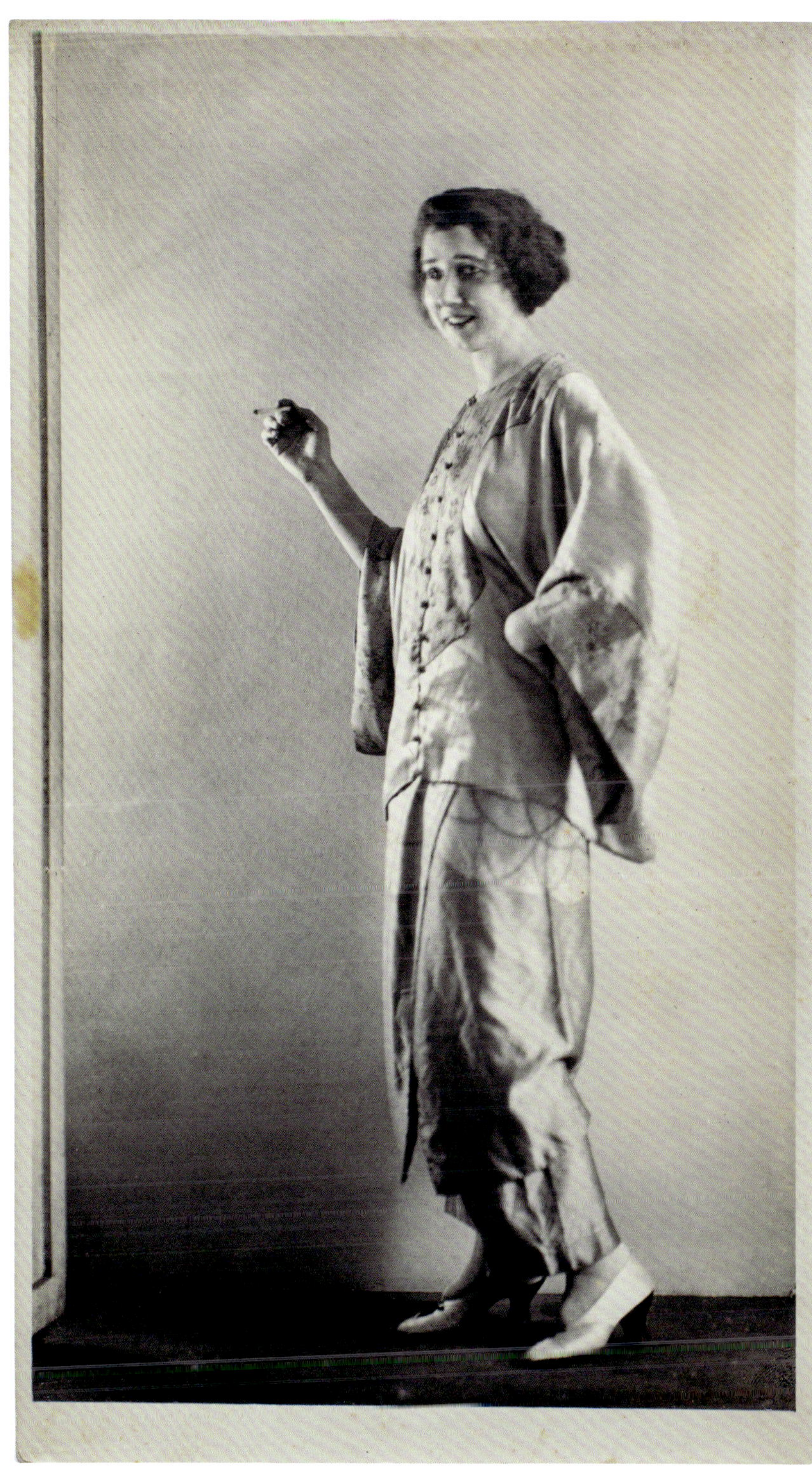

Don Rafael Gonzalez Abreu y Lopez Silvero—Ethel's Rafo, her Great
Cat, her Washington Square Cat, her Lion, in her words—was her intellectual equal and creative inspiration. Their initial encounter likely
occurred in 1914, during one of the periodic stops Abreu made in New
York while traveling between Spain and his home country of Cuba.[54]
His departure left her "haunted with the beauty and fire" of his conver-
sation.[55] Throughout the next two decades, the two would keep in contact via letters and meet in person when they could, but Abreu, at least,

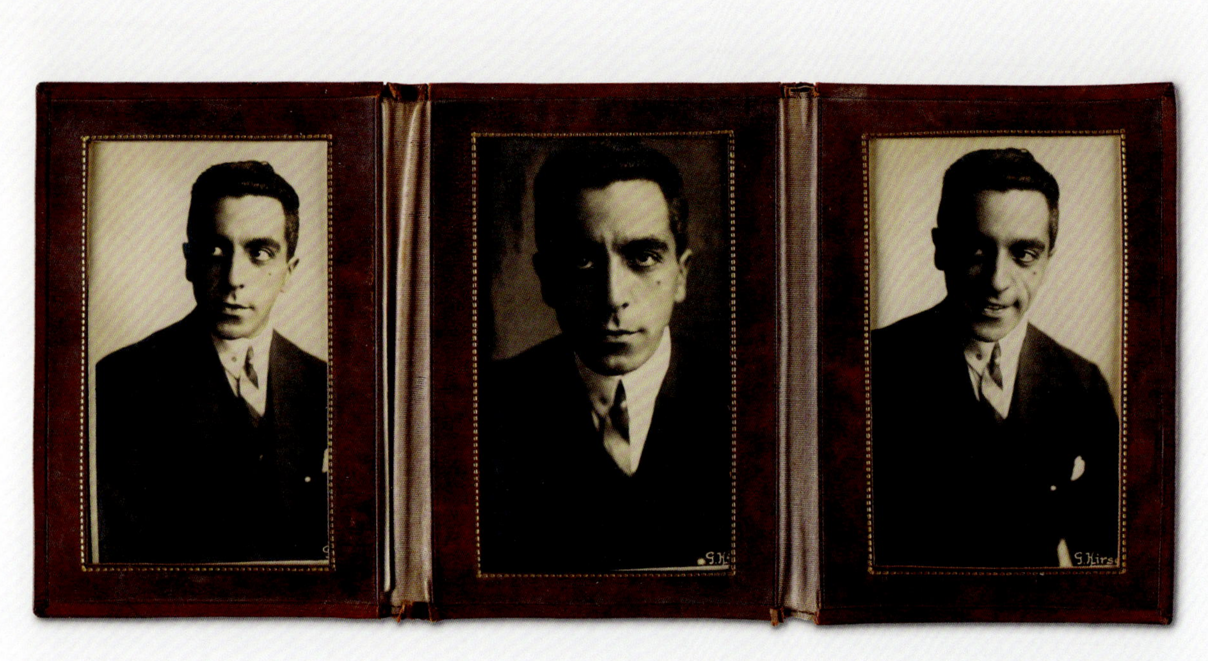

FIG. 39
Unknown photographer, *Portraits of Rafael Abreu*, n.d. Photographs, 5⅛ × 3½ inches (each); 6 × 12⅞ inches (framed). Ethel Wallace papers. Collection of the late Kristina Barbara Johnson, courtesy of Jeniah Johnson.

resisted commitment, presumably due to their distance and age difference (he was twenty years her senior), as well as the fact that Wallace was still legally married to Nat Roberts. In a letter draft to Abreu, she teases him for his fusty principles:

> A sad fairy must have come at my birth & said—she shall have always to love & long to see Rafo—talented & brilliant men will bring their love and she will be foolish enough to turn aside to cry "I want to see Rafo I want to see Rafo" & in spite of your life & me sounding conceited to say it I think you love me more than any—you are bothered because I am American & a poor independent person with my own ideas & as a man—& you have an inherited Spanish stubbornness that makes you tenacious to a passion . . . —you cling to your age—being perhaps afraid of beginning your youth again with a modern person who insists on you being modern spiritually & mentally.[56]

Creatively, Wallace was most inspired by Abreu to write. Regaled with colorful stories from his life in Cuba and Spain and captivated by the unfair trial and execution of a Hispanic man that occurred in Bucks County in the nineteenth century, she wrote a play for Abreu titled *The Beggar's Room*, which blended their cultural backgrounds, advocated for fair treatment of people of color, and criticized the United States' prejudiced judicial system. In her introduction to that play, she wrote of its inspiration, "I was reminded of a friend . . . I thought if this man, Don Rafael, by some odd chance were to come to Bucks County today . . . even he could be destroyed by the trinity of disbelief, prejudice and

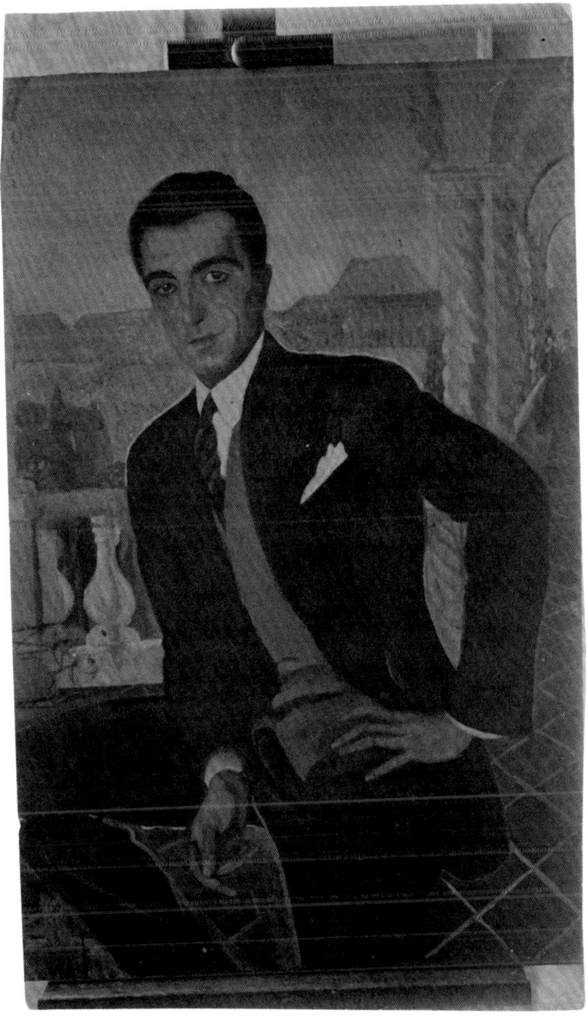

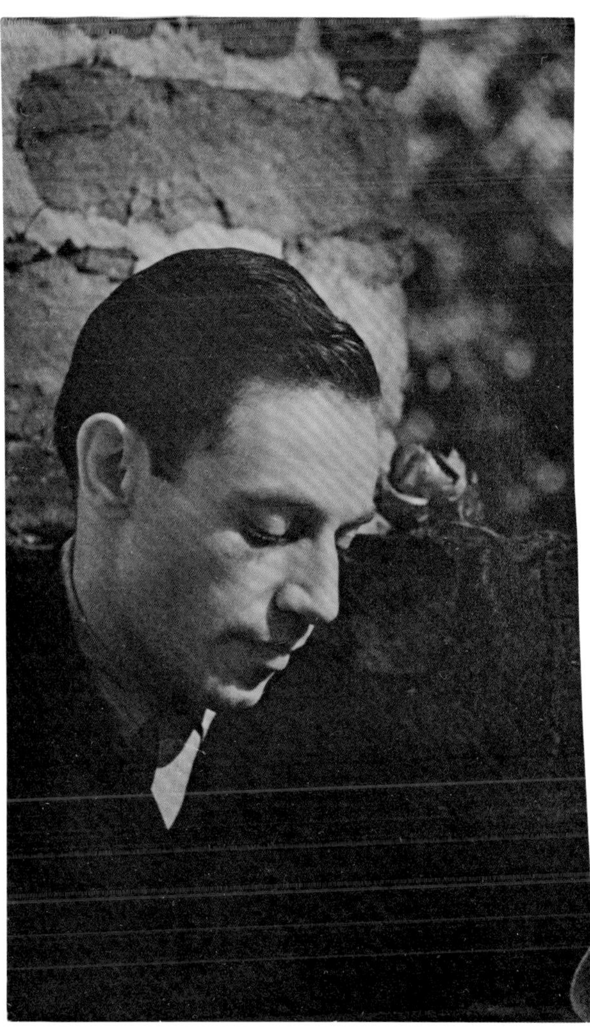

ignorance."[57] Despite her efforts to promote the play, it never reached the stage, either due to the usual lack of interest or because of its searing criticism of racism and injustice. Wallace wrote poetry for Abreu, too, including one sultry poem titled "Prayer to the Great Cat."

It was likely during her visit to Spain in 1920 to study European art that her visual work was most influenced by Abreu, whose brother owned an impressive collection of Spanish paintings (Fig. 42). Enamored with El Greco and inspired by Francisco de Goya, Wallace painted upon her return to Pennsylvania her own version of Goya's *The Naked Maja* (Figs. 43 and 44), a painting in which a nude Venus lies provocatively on a pile of cushions. Wallace's *Maja* (a Spanish term for brazenly dressed, lower-class citizens), though closely modeled after the original, most noticeably differs from Goya's in the fact that hers is Black. It is possible that this change was a practical one, as Wallace mentions in her letters a Black woman named Louise who often modeled for her paintings.[58] Even so, the painting sexualizes the woman as an exoticized Black alternative to Goya's white European subject, and Wallace's plan for the painting was equally provocative. Intending to gift the work to Abreu, she included in her composition a subtle, flirtatious message: the woman, who stands in for the Roman goddess of love and sex, lounges upon a chaise carved into

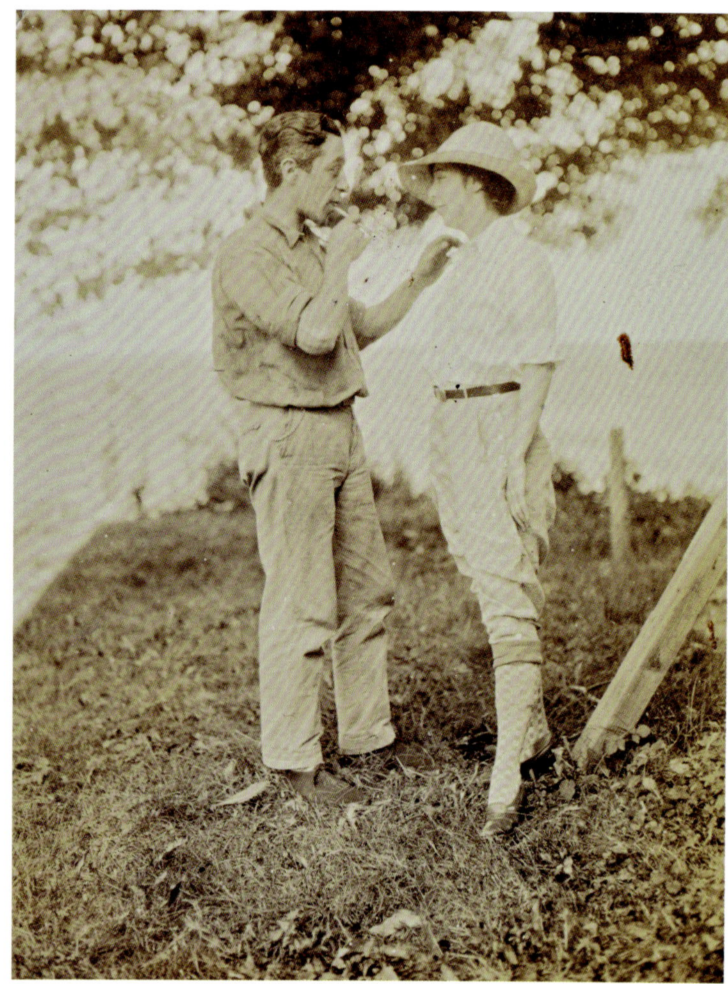

the shape of a lion—a Great Cat. In another letter draft to Abreu, Wallace writes, "I have finished my Maja Negra. Rose O'Neil [*sic*] says it is the most beautiful thing I have done."[59] Wallace intended to take the painting, along with another planned (though never completed) painting titled *A Madonna of the Bulls*, to Abreu in Spain, but her return trip was delayed due to the Depression's impact on her finances, and in 1933, she received a letter from his nephew informing her of his death. Her papers contain several multipage, emotionally written letter drafts in response, in which she expresses her anguish over the news:

> It was kind of you to write to me. It was a terrible shock for your uncle Rafael Abreu was to me everything—because in some mysterious way from that first moment when he was brought to my studio in New York he influenced rather completely my thoughts & work—I did not assimilate it all however until these last few years when with my back against the wall I have fought all kinds of horrors that the condition of this country has brought about & thanks to that pouring out of *his* mind & heart I find the art in me. Now I do not know—I feel that his death breaks the heart of any creative power I have.[60]

48

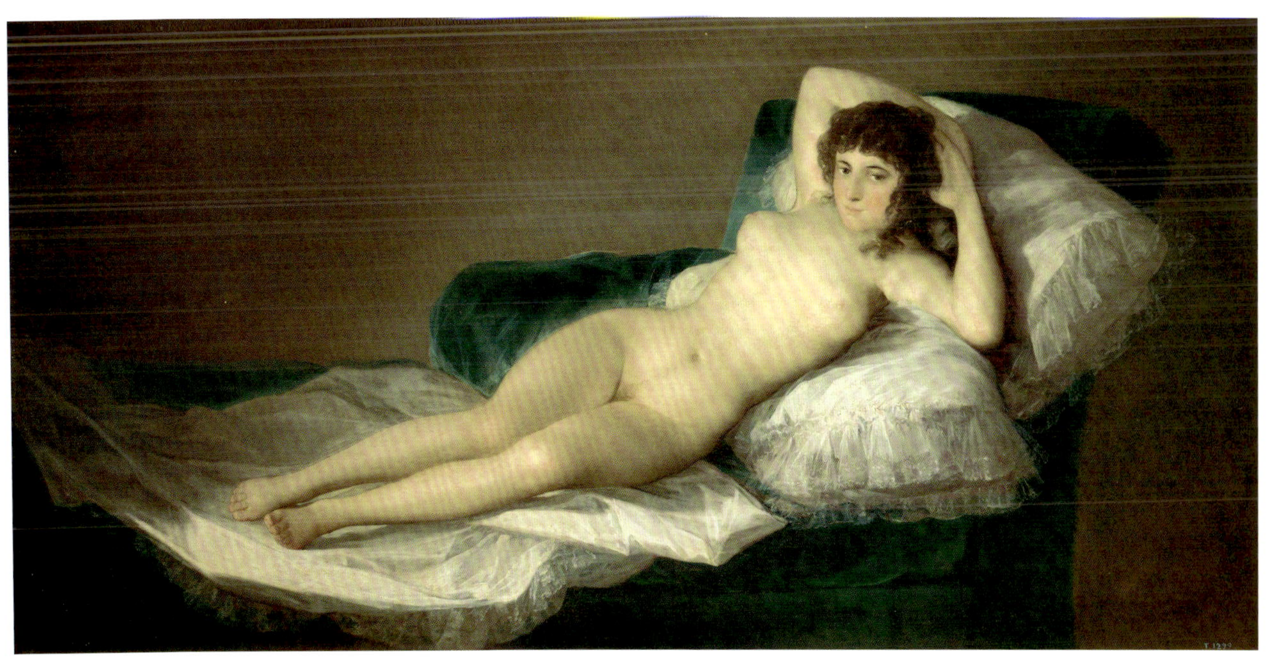

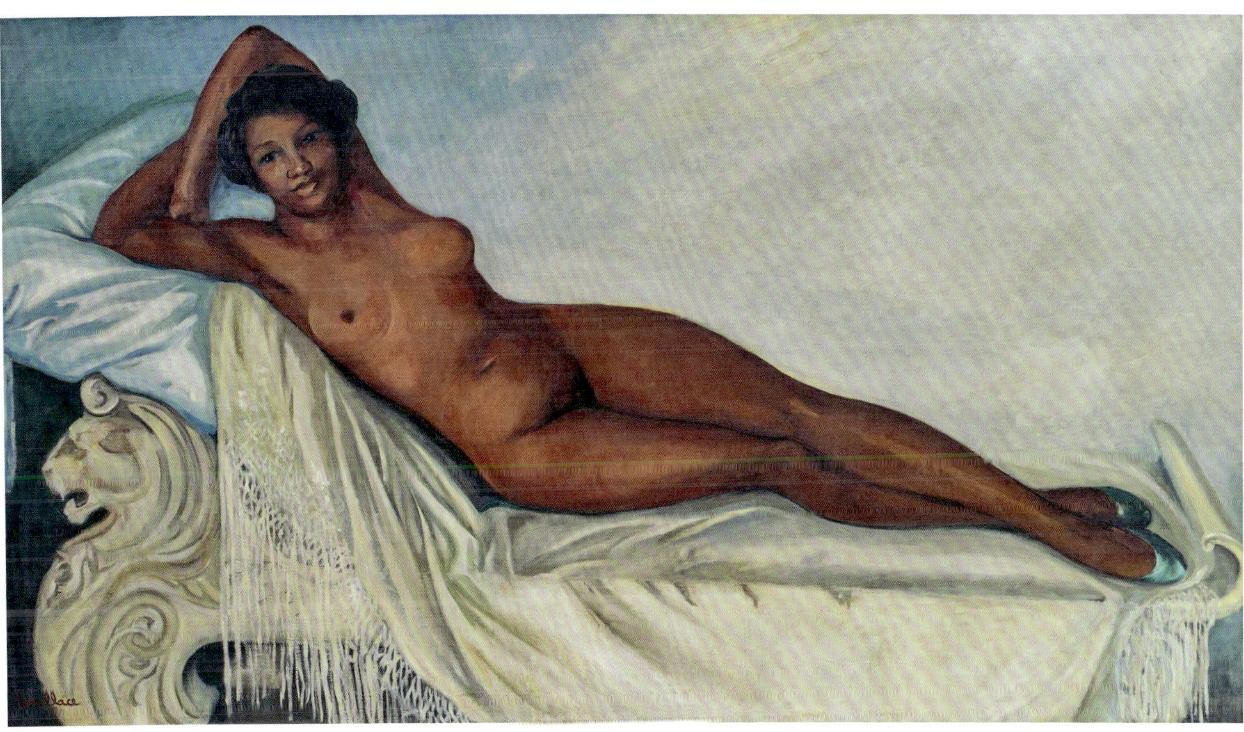

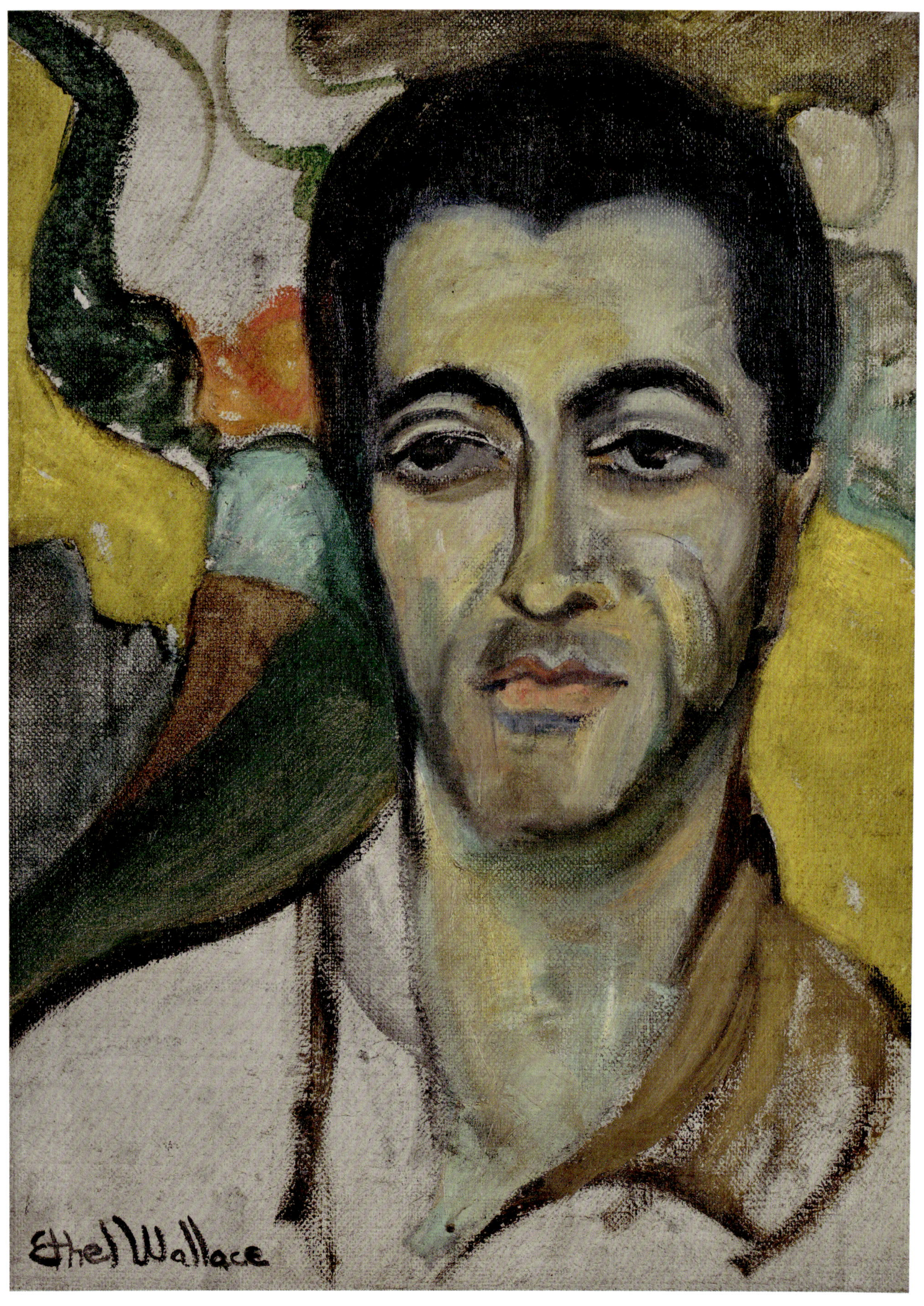
Ethel Wallace

Ethel Wallace (1886–1968), *Untitled (Portrait of Rafael Abreu)*, n.d. Oil on canvas, 20 × 15 inches. Collection of the late Kristina Barbara Johnson, courtesy of Jeniah Johnson.

Wallace held on to photographs of Abreu for the next thirty-five years of her life. They are now a part of the material she left behind, along with an undated portrait she painted of him, either from life or from one of her photographs (Fig. 45). The portrait presents Abreu—her Rafo—with deep-set, thoughtful eyes and strong laugh lines. He sits before a background swirling with emotive color.

By the time Abreu died, Wallace had been living back in Bucks County for several years. A fire in 1925 burned down the building where her shop was located, and around this same time, she and Roberts reunited and purchased the property of her father's old grist mill in Lambertville.[61] Wallace worked there at least part-time for a few years, splitting her time between the mill studio and New York until she moved to Bucks County permanently in 1930. Roberts still traveled often for work, and that same year, he fell ill while abroad and died on his way back to the United States. The timing could not have been worse. Without her shop, the proximity of her clientele, or the support of the Parisian couturiers to whom she tried to sell her designs, Wallace's income evaporated at the exact time the Great Depression hit the US economy. Abreu's death came three years later, and her mental health plummeted. In letters to playwright John Balderston, a friend and another possible lover, she writes of her "constant condition" of "sick dismay and the sensation of dropping dropping."[62] She also addresses her financial difficulties and fatigue toward work and writing correspondence:

> Please never put me down in your thoughts as my silences
> seem to deserve. Sometimes I'm literally paralyzed as far as
> getting things done—& always interruptions—I can never
> get away from people not so much friends, there are lots of
> them too, but somehow people of all ages classes & sexes
> tell me their stories or pass the time of day. At a time like this
> when I stay alive by credit alone, & hold the few possessions
> I have until they can be turned into cash—this has been an
> asset for protection, though not for work or the things I am
> most interested in. And it makes for a really terrible fatigue.[63]

Like women who pursued careers as artists, mental health was not taken as seriously in Wallace's era as it is today. Her financial difficulties only worsened her health, as they limited her ability to work. She wrote to a friend, "Betty wants to buy one of the silk decorations—but people want low prices. However I'm trying to finish up some still life—but my paints are all so old & dried up it takes twice as long to paint."[64] A letter from the Philadelphia Art Alliance, a popular venue for local artists looking to exhibit their work, gives a glimpse into Wallace's attempts to maintain her career's momentum amid the Depression:

> My dear Ethel: Thank you very much for your note con-
> cerning your account with the Art Alliance. Please feel free
> to cover it at your convenience. I am so sorry to hear of

your difficulties, and I do hope they will soon be over. I felt
as badly as you did that there were no sales, but I believe
the exhibition was valuable in keeping your name before
the public and that is particularly important at a time like
this, although there may not be any tangible results. The
next time I come to New Hope, I shall be only too happy to
come to see you and in the meantime—my very warm hopes
that the tide is turning.[65]

Despite her depression and impoverishment, Wallace still displayed her usual enchanting personality, maintained lifelong friendships,
and continued to write, paint, and promote her work when she could.
She exhibited several times with New Hope's modernist art group, first
founded in 1930 under the name "the New Group" by Charles Ramsey after his friend, artist Lloyd Ney, was rejected from the Phillips' Mill
Annual Exhibition in New Hope. The Mill exhibitions typically displayed
work by the region's impressionists, including William Lathrop, who
reportedly deemed Ney's boldly colorful painting unsuitable for the
venue. The decision inspired local modernists to exhibit their work in
alternative venues, including their own gallery, the Independent, though
they continued to exhibit at Phillips' Mill, too. In an article about Wallace
in a local newspaper, Ramsey describes his impression of her:

> Ethel Wallace did not find herself until she got into the
> study of actual transcription of subject—her academic view-
> point had her fettered; she was freed by her excursions into
> design and color. In this process of freeing herself from
> academic fetters, she was aided by the use of a beautiful
> medium of expression—namely, painting with wax and dyes.
> She now goes back to oils, no longer hampered by her early
> academic training; rules kill personality. She now shows a
> freer expression, completely personal.[66]

Though Ramsey mentions her return to oils with a "freer expression" than her early, impressionist work, whatever modern paintings
she was producing have now either been lost or secluded within private
collections.

One review of an exhibition held at New Hope's Independent Gallery at least alludes to the subject matter she was pursuing:

> [Wallace's] *Construction Work in New York City*, with its
> murky pink sky, has the same charm, while her arrangement
> of dahlias, seen against a mirror, has a very positive quality,
> with an agreeable disregard of details, and reveals the subtle
> sense of color which makes all her work so intensely inter-
> esting. It does not matter whether the other candlestick is
> painted or not. Its presence is as completely registered as if
> it were.[67]

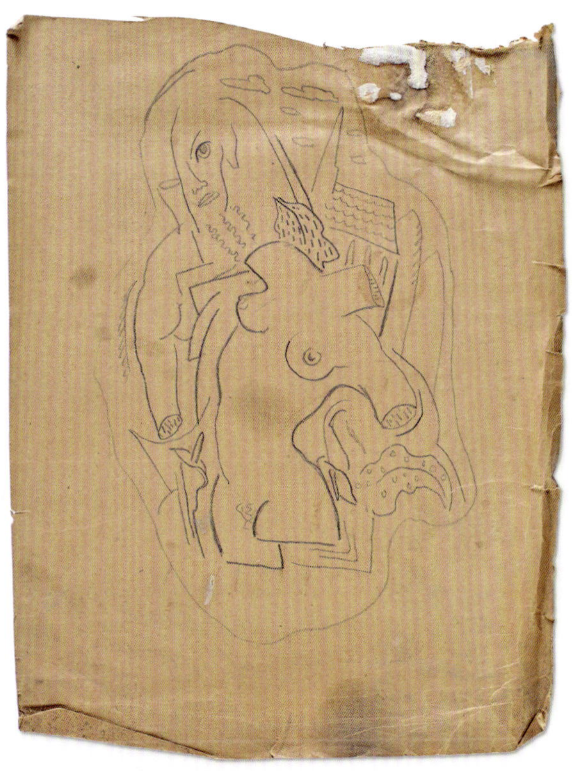

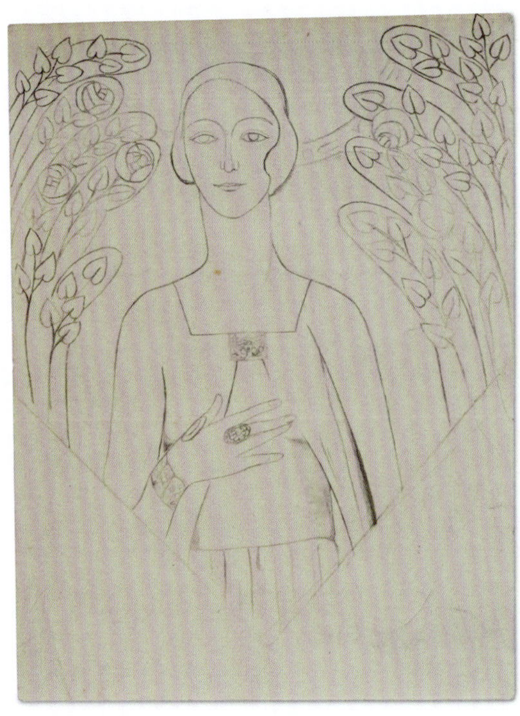

The New York scene was likely an earlier painting produced during her time in the city, and as such it confirms her previous attention to the changing urban landscape. The dahlias, meanwhile, with their mirrored background and simplified candlestick, imply her experimentation with materials, abstraction, and expressive brushstrokes. Sketches found in her papers show her explorations of simplified and cubist forms, for which she studied and took notes on the work of Juan Gris, Robert Delaunay, and Marcel Duchamp (Figs. 46 and 47).[68]

The review of the exhibition at the Independent Gallery also states that the featured artists were "different individuals who are not identified with any particular coterie, but who prefer to maintain their independence."[69] Along with Wallace's work, the exhibition featured the paintings of Fern Coppedge, another local woman artist whose bright palettes and brushy canvases offered an innovative and experimental approach to impressionism. Coppedge was also a member of the Philadelphia Ten, a women's artist group that Wallace never joined.[70] Whether she abhorred the thought of exhibiting her work under the label of "artist woman," as one journalist once eloquently described Wallace,[71] or she just was not interested, the fact remains that she was always, stubbornly, her own person.

In her later years, Wallace tried to make money with her writing, but her plays were never produced (Fig. 48). She reverted to her earlier, brushier, pastel style of painting, either with the hope of selling the work to the area's conservative clientele or simply because it came naturally

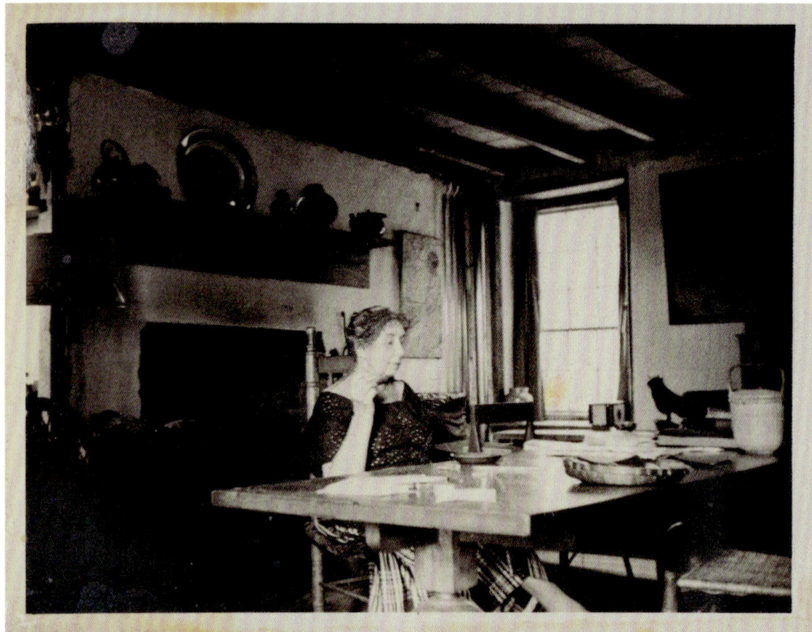

FIG. 48
Unknown photographer, *Ethel in Her Home*, n.d. Photograph, 3¹⁵⁄₁₆ × 4¹⁵⁄₁₆ inches. Ethel Wallace papers. Collection of the late Kristina Barbara Johnson, courtesy of Jeniah Johnson.

FIG. 49
Ethel Wallace (1886–1968), *Untitled (Floral Still Life)*, n.d. Oil on canvas, 29 × 47½ inches (framed). Collection of Frederick Schillinger.

and made her happy. In yet another letter to a friend, she wrote, "I've been painting flowers again—I go rather drunk with spring flowers."[72] She reportedly kept a marvelous garden that offered endless opportunities for creative release, and when she wasn't painting flowers, she turned her attention to her darling cats—one of which was named Laurence Olivier (Figs. 49–52).

Despite the craze her batiks inspired, her paintings never achieved the same success. In the fifty-five years since her death, Wallace has been lost to the history of modernism, relegated to the ranks of Linda Nochlin's forgotten flower painters.[73] Considering she was active at a time when women artists had to fight to be taken seriously, I wonder if Wallace's work in textiles was more widely accepted by critics of both genders simply because textiles were a medium deemed more appropriate for women. Had she lived in an era less riddled with sexism and economic depression, she may have continued to develop her skills and style in both media, and her career may not have ended early, and in obscurity. In spite of this, she was inarguably a part of modernist movements in both New York and New Hope. Though much of her work has faded or been lost, her life and the images

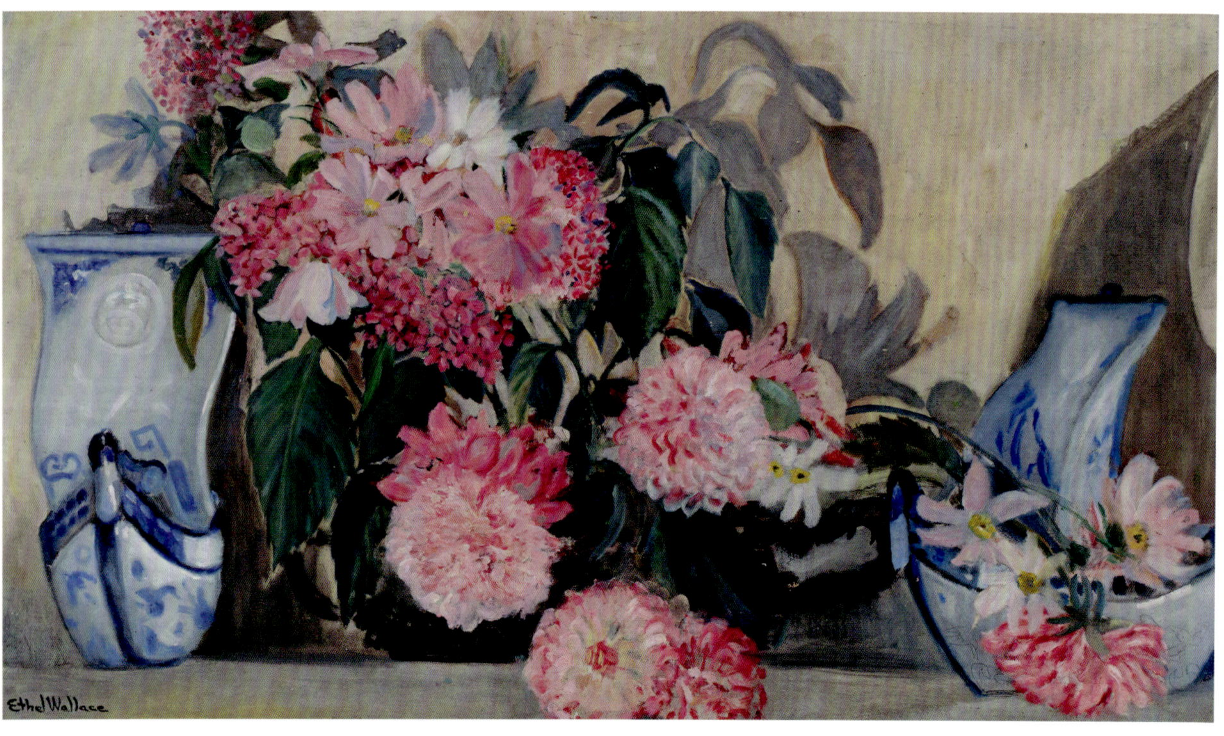

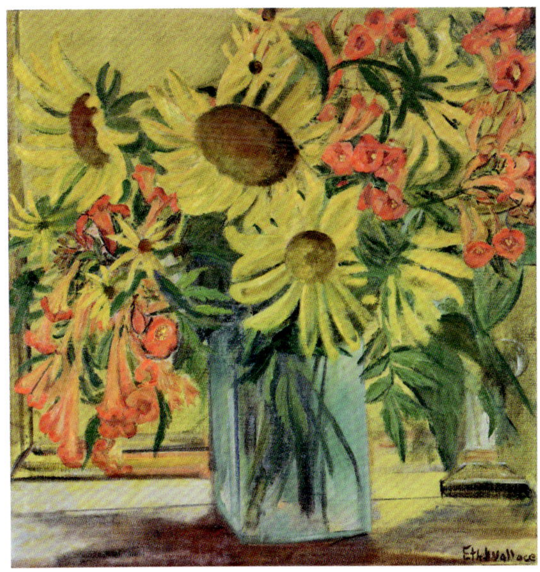 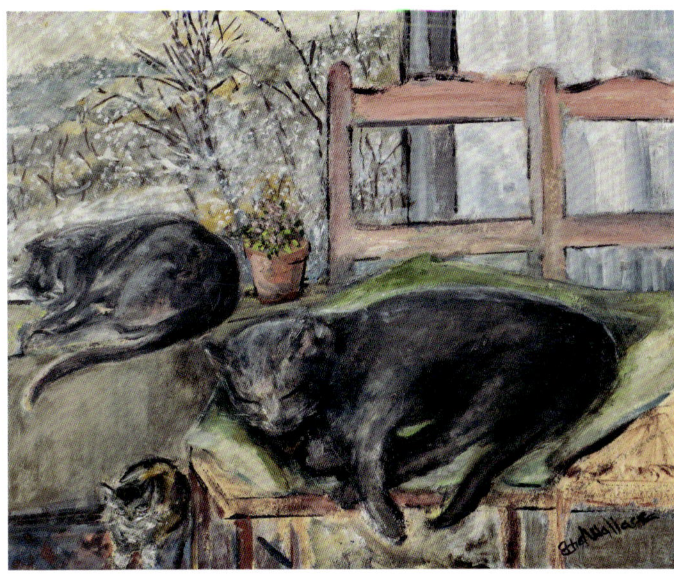

FIG. 50
Ethel Wallace (1886–1968), *Untitled (Floral Still Life)*, n.d. Oil on canvas, 41 × 40 inches (framed). Collection of Edwin Hild.

FIG. 51
Ethel Wallace (1886–1968), *Untitled (Cats)*, n.d. Oil on canvas, 16 × 20 inches. Collection of the late Kristina Barbara Johnson, courtesy of Jeniah Johnson.

FIG. 52
Ethel Wallace (1886–1968), *Bambouli*, 1964. Pencil on paper, 4½ × 7 inches. Ethel Wallace papers. Collection of the late Kristina Barbara Johnson, courtesy of Jeniah Johnson.

she created capture an iconic, volatile age of opulence and recession, global conflict and innovation.

In a 1933 edition of the *New Hope*, an article on the town's recent happenings mentions Ethel: "The river still flows past Lambertville and Ethel Wallace still trudges across the bridge to her studio where her genius resolves itself into colorful batiks."[74] And so she lingers in legend, on the same bridge where she used to watch moonlight reflect on water; or on the dance floor, twisting in a tango with a friend she called Panther; or freewheeling her way through town in a beater with no windshield, curls tousled by the breeze.

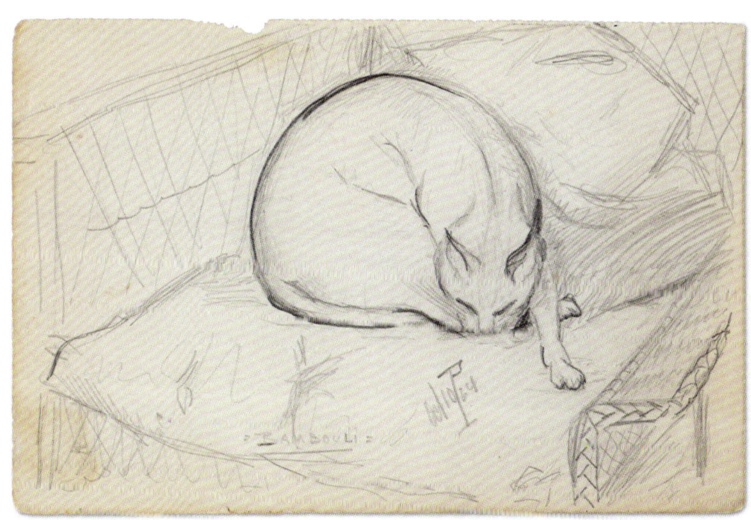

The epigraph is from undated notes found in the Ethel Wallace papers, collection of the late Kristina Barbara Johnson.

1. "Ethel Is Gone," *Bucks County Gazette*, November 21, 1968, 1.

2. Mike Ellis, "So Ungiving Are People . . . Except in the Case of Ethel," *Bucks County Gazette*, November 21, 1968, 14.

3. Mike Ellis, postcard to the artist, 1968, Ethel Wallace papers.

4. Ethel Wallace to Rafael Abreu, n.d., Ethel Wallace papers.

5. Eleanor Miller, interview with the author, October 26, 2022.

6. Brenda Meredith, interview with the author, May 31, 2022.

7. Brian H. Peterson, "Impressionism Comes to Bucks County: The Story of the New Hope Art Colony," in *Pennsylvania Impressionism*, ed. Brian H. Peterson (Doylestown, PA: Michener Art Museum; Philadelphia: University of Pennsylvania Press, 2002), 3–5.

8. The work has previously (and mistakenly) been referred to as *Prudential Building, Philadelphia*, but its subject matter depicts New York City's Woolworth Building. In the painting, the Woolworth's unlit windows suggest that Wallace may have studied this scene prior to the tower's opening ceremony on April 24, 1913, when President Woodrow Wilson pressed a button from the White House to illuminate each of its windows at once.

9. Barbara Haskell, "The Last Flourish of the Gilded Age," in *The American Century: Art and Culture, 1900–1950* (exhibition catalogue) (New York: Whitney Museum of American Art, 1999), 47.

10. Charles S. Marlor, *The Society of Independent Artists: The Exhibition Record, 1917–1944* (Park Ridge, NJ: Noyes Press, 1984), 560.

11. Despite the efforts of those involved in the show, the money from sales did not reach the campaign, and women's right to vote in New York was not won until 1917.

12. *Exhibition of Painting and Sculpture by Women Artists for the Benefit of the Woman Suffrage Campaign* (exhibition catalogue), 1915, bulk 1915–1925, box 3, folder 26, item 1, Miscellaneous art exhibition catalogue collection, 1813–1953, Archives of American Art, Smithsonian Institution, Washington, DC.

13. Laura R. Prieto, "Gallery Scrapbook as Suffrage Archive: Macbeth's Suffrage Exhibition," *Archives of American Art Journal* 60, no. 1 (Spring 2021): 8–9, 18.

14. Anna Marley, "In the City: The Progressive Era and the New Women of Philadelphia," in *Women in Motion: 150 Years of Women's Artistic Networks at the Pennsylvania Academy of the Fine Arts* (exhibition catalogue) (Philadelphia: Pennsylvania Academy of the Fine Arts, 2021), 32; Laura R. Prieto, *At Home in the Studio: The Professionalization of Women Artists in America* (Cambridge, MA: Harvard University Press, 2001); Page Talbott and Patricia Tanis Sydney, *The Philadelphia Ten: A Women's Artist Group, 1917–1945* (Philadelphia: Moore College of Art and Design; Kansas City, MO: American Art Review Press, 1998).

15. Ethel Wallace, undated notes, Ethel Wallace papers.

16. Ethel Wallace, undated notes, Ethel Wallace papers.

17. Harrison Rhodes, "The Reviewing Stand," *Town and Country*, December 15, 1921, 34.

18. Ethel Wallace, undated notes, Ethel Wallace papers.

19. Haskell, "The Last Flourish of the Gilded Age," 31.

20. Mandy Cooper, "Life at Trinity College during the Great War," *Duke University Libraries* (Fall/Winter 2018–19), https://blogs.library.duke.edu/magazine/2019/01/11/since-the-war-began-times-aint-what-they-used-to-be/.

21. "Blue Devils March, Broadway Hoarse: Three Mile Throng Extends Wild Greeting to Poilus and Americans," *New York Sun*, May 1, 1918, 16.

22. Ethel Wallace, undated correspondence, Ethel Wallace papers.

23. "Sensational Art Being Displayed This Month at Columbus Gallery," *Ohio State Journal*, January 15, 1928.

24. *12th Annual Exhibition of Paintings and Sculpture* (exhibition catalogue) (New York: Whitney Studio Club, 1927), Ethel Wallace scrapbook, Ethel Wallace papers.

25. "Woman Artist Makes Batik: Miss Ethel Wallace Has Created 2,500 Yards of Fabric," *Daily Garment News*, January 5, 1920; Frederick Lau, "Java to Jazz: Eva Gauthier," in Henry Spiller, *Javaphilia: American Love Affairs with Javanese Music and Dance* (Honolulu: University of Hawaii Press, 2015), 56. Gauthier did not perform true Javanese folk songs. According to Lau, "For Eva Gauthier, Javanese music—or at least an orientalist simulacrum of Javanese music that was convincing to her American audiences—provided the key she needed to self-fashion a coherent subjectivity from her heterogeneous life experiences" ("Java to Jazz," 87). For more on Gauthier, see Michael Mamp's essay in this catalogue.

26. Abby G. Lillethun, "Batik in America: Javanese to Javanesque, 1893 to 1937" (PhD diss., Ohio State University, 2002), 74–79.

27. Lillethun, "Batik in America," 71–118.

28. Nicola J. Shilliam, "From Bohemian to Bourgeois: American Batik in the Early Twentieth Century," in *Contact, Crossover, Continuity: Proceedings of the Fourth Biennial Symposium of the Textile Society of America, September 22–24, 1994* (Los Angeles: Textile Society of America, Inc., 1995), 254–55, https://digitalcommons.unl.edu/tsaconf/1052.

29. Shilliam, "From Bohemian to Bourgeois," 255.

30. Shilliam, "From Bohemian to Bourgeois," 255.

31. Ethel Wallace, undated correspondence, Ethel Wallace papers. By "warmer," Wallace means the vat of warm water in

which she would dip the newly dyed textiles to melt the wax from them.

32. Lillethun, "Batik in America," 10.

33. Lillethun, "Batik in America," 53.

34. "Pioneer in Batik Portraits," *Evening News* (Harrisburg, PA), December 22, 1921, 18.

35. "Woman Artist Makes Batik."

36. One photo shows Wallace using a paintbrush in lieu of the traditional Javanese tjanting, a pen-shaped tool used to draw a design with melted wax on cloth. Based on this photo and a close study of Wallace's batiks, which show evidence of pencil sketches, it is likely that she regularly used pencils and paintbrushes in her process, which would have made it easier to achieve her signature, smooth lines. The photo is reproduced in "New Idea," *Daily News* (New York), November 14, 1921.

37. Susan A. Glenn, "The Americanization of Salome: Sexuality, Race, and the Careers of the Vulgar Princess," in *Female Spectacle: The Theatrical Roots of Modern Feminism* (Cambridge, MA: Harvard University Press, 2002), 99.

38. Glenn, "The Americanization of Salome," 99.

39. Glenn, "The Americanization of Salome," 96.

40. Quoted in Glenn, "The Americanization of Salome," 96.

41. Donald Gorley, "Ethel Wallace: Gay Primitive," *International Studio*, February 1923, 381.

42. *Town and Country*, May 1921, Ethel Wallace scrapbook, Ethel Wallace papers.

43. "She'll Do You in Batik, the Newest Rage in Art," *New Castle Herald*, December 14, 1921; *Vogue Paris*, July 1921, 15.

44. Ethel Wallace scrapbook, Ethel Wallace papers.

45. "Woman's World and Its Ways," *Evening Standard* (London), July 24, 1920.

46. "Woman Artist Makes Batik."

47. Einav Rabinovitch-Fox, "(Re)Fashioning the New Woman: Women's Dress, the Oriental Style, and the Construction of American Feminist Imagery in the 1910s," *Journal of Women's History* 27, no. 2 (2015): 17.

48. Rabinovitch-Fox, "(Re)Fashioning the New Woman," 17–19.

49. Rabinovitch-Fox, "(Re)Fashioning the New Woman," 15.

50. Rabinovitch-Fox, "(Re)Fashioning the New Woman," 15.

51. "Portraits of Men May Adorn Gowns," *Providence Journal*, March 21, 1922, Ethel Wallace scrapbook, Ethel Wallace papers.

52. Michael Mamp, "Ethel Wallace: A Forgotten History of Batik and Fashion," *Journal of Modern Craft* 14, no. 3 (2021): 253–73, DOI: 10.1080/17496772.2021.2000706.

53. In 1928, Abreu's founding of Seville, Spain's Hispano-Cuban Institute of American History prompted King Alfonso III to grant him the noble title of Viscount of Los Remedios. (Los Remedios is the neighborhood in Seville where he lived.) He was also decorated with the Grand Cross of the Civil Order of Alfonso XII.

54. Ancestry, "List or Manifest of Alien Passengers for the United States, Cadiz to New York (August 26, 1914)," 86.

55. Ethel Wallace, undated note, Ethel Wallace papers.

56. Ethel Wallace to Rafael Abreu, n.d., Ethel Wallace papers.

57. Ethel Wallace, introduction to *The Beggar's Room*, n.d., Ethel Wallace papers.

58. Ethel Wallace, undated note, Ethel Wallace papers.

59. Ethel Wallace to Rafael Abreu, n.d., Ethel Wallace papers. O'Neill was an American illustrator and writer whose cartoon character, Kewpie, became an international sensation and icon of the suffrage movement. O'Neill moved from her home state of Nebraska to New York, where she purchased an apartment in Washington Square, near Wallace's studio. The two likely met through their proximity, their involvement in New York's artist circles, and their work for suffrage.

60. Ethel Wallace to nephew of Rafael Abreu, ca. 1933, Ethel Wallace papers.

61. Wallace financial records, Ethel Wallace papers.

62. Ethel Wallace to John Balderston, n.d., Ethel Wallace papers.

63. Ethel Wallace to John Balderston, n.d., Ethel Wallace papers.

64. Ethel Wallace to unknown recipient, n.d., Ethel Wallace papers.

65. Clara R. Mason to Ethel Wallace, ca. 1931, Ethel Wallace papers.

66. Quoted in Gee See, "Folks Worth Knowing in the Delaware Valley: Ethel Wallace, Who Rejuvenated and Developed an Ancient Art to 'Find' Herself," *New Hope News*, December 19, 1929.

67. "Women at the Independent," *New Hope: A Record of the Contemporary American Arts* 2, no. 5 (September 1934): 3.

68. Ethel Wallace papers.

69. "Women at the Independent," 3.

70. Talbott and Sydney, *The Philadelphia Ten*, 84–90.

71. Ethel Wallace papers.

72. Ethel Wallace to unknown recipient, n.d., Ethel Wallace papers.

73. Nochlin's 1971 essay "Why Have There Been No Great Women Artists" criticized art history's patriarchal narrative and failure to address the societal structures that for centuries denied women education and careers. Their limited opportunities caused whatever work women artists made—which often reflected the domestic space and activities they were restricted to, like textile work and floral still lifes—to be lost to history. Linda Nochlin, *Why Have There Been No Great Women Artists?* (London: Thames & Hudson, 2021).

74. "News," *New Hope: Written for and by Residents of the Delaware Valley* 1, no. 3 (October 1933): 18.

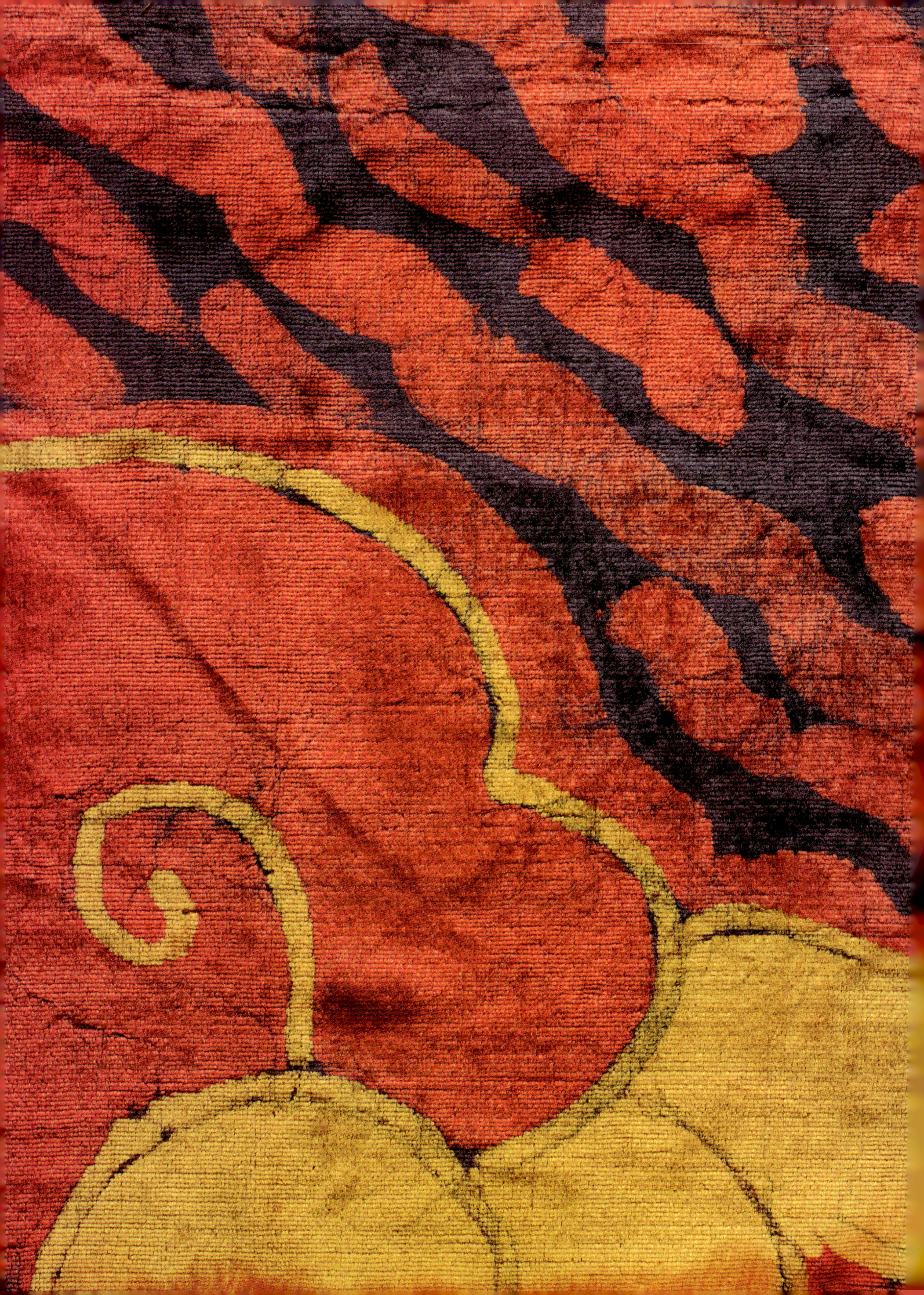

Ethel Wallace
FASHIONING BATIK

Michael Mamp

I FIRST BECAME AWARE OF ETHEL WALLACE about twelve years ago when I saw her portrait of the famous modernist French couturier Paul Poiret. My husband, a longtime Bucks County resident, interior designer, and art collector, had purchased the portrait in Lambertville, New Jersey, at the gallery of Roy Pedersen years earlier. Being a fashion and textile historian, I was intrigued; who was this woman, and how was she connected to the King of Fashion himself? In my quest to learn more about Ethel Wallace, I interviewed Pedersen; antique dealer Mary K. Darrah; Phillips' Mill member Eleanor Miller; and the Farley family of Farley's Bookshop in New Hope, Pennsylvania, who bought Wallace's house after her passing in 1968. I soon learned that Wallace lore was plentiful in and around New Hope. People enthusiastically regaled me with stories of lemon butter, peyote tea, love affairs, and Wallace's modern rebel spirit. However, accessing her work and source material suitable for academic research was challenging. My husband once participated in a show house for the Junior League of Greater Princeton, where he designed a kitchen in which the Poiret portrait was hung. He remembered a beautiful, stylish woman who walked through the room and said, "I used to own that!" That woman was Kristina Barbara Johnson; luckily, Roy Pedersen had her phone number. Thus began a multiyear process of attempted but failed communication.

"Hello, Kristina, it's Michael Mamp; I was hoping to speak to you today about Ethel Wallace"—*No, not today*—"OK, well, how about Tuesday?"—*You could try!* Kristina and I never met, but we spoke on

59

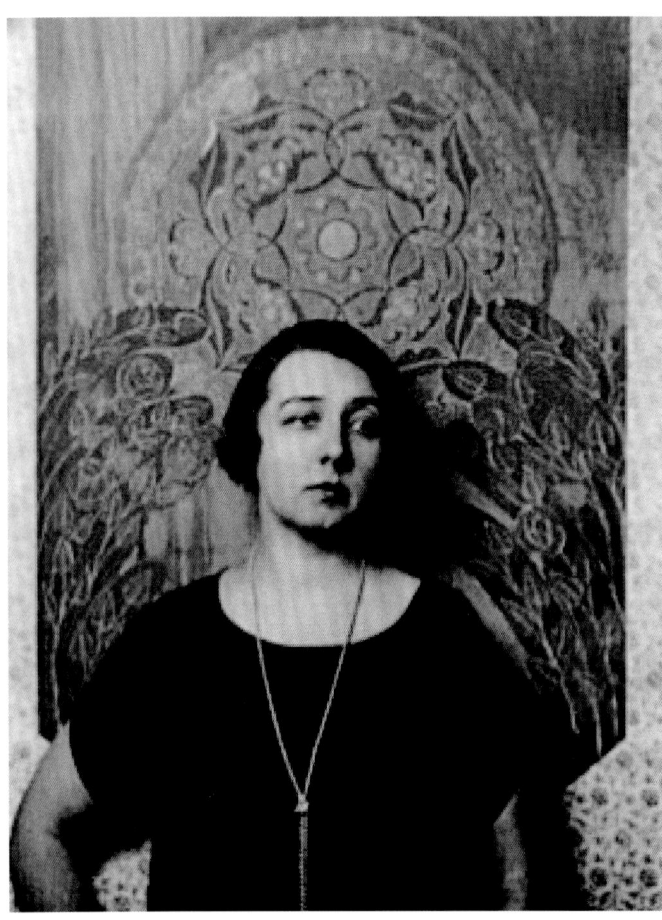

the phone several times in cat-and-mouse staccato conversations. She had three questions she asked me repeatedly: *Do you like beets? What is your astrological sign?* And: *Are you a Democrat?* This back-and-forth went on for a few years. Perhaps I never answered correctly, or Kristina was just not up to having visitors, but sadly, she passed away in 2013 before we could meet in person. Shortly after her mother's death, Jeniah Johnson discovered my letters and voice mails and reached out. She generously granted me access to the complete archive of Wallace's papers and ephemera. Summarizing the history of Wallace's batik-making was not easy, as very few of the textiles survive into the present. Two of her scrapbooks served as my primary source material, and the story slowly emerged.[1]

Ethel Wallace (1886–1968) was an artist, designer, and maker who worked in various media from the early to mid-twentieth century (Fig. 1).[2] In the 1920s, she gained acclaim for her textiles created using the batik method, exhibiting her work across the United States and abroad. Batik, a wax-resist dyeing method for cloth, gained popularity in the early twentieth century. The process aligned with the American Arts and Crafts movement, which emphasized "the virtues of handmade objects."[3] Generally, "the underlying principle of wax-resist dyeing is that those parts of the cloth to remain undyed are covered with molten wax . . . [and] in Javanese batik, wax is applied by hand with a small instrument called the canting."[4] While differing methods of wax-resist dyeing of textiles have existed throughout history and around the world, the technique is often associated with the Indonesian island of Java in the South Pacific.[5] It was the Javanese interpretation that prompted a batik revival in the Western world in the late nineteenth and early twentieth centuries. During this revival, Wallace gained prominence for her batik "paintings" of portraits on cloth. According to Wallace, "I believe textile painting may be the medium of artistic expression of the *modern* age."[6] In addition to portraits, she made wall hangings that featured mythical, nature, or biblical scenes and thousands of yards of fabric used for fashion.

After moving to New York City in the late 1910s, Wallace was introduced to batik by her friend, opera singer Éva Gauthier. Gauthier lived in Java for several years and was enamored with the culture. When she moved to New York in 1914, she advanced her career as a soloist with a repertoire that included westernized interpretations of Javanese songs. Gauthier had a rudimentary understanding of the culture supplemented by her library research and presented this appropriated Javanese culture as authentic.[7] According to anthropologist Matthew Isaac Cohen, Gauthier went from "second-rate opera singer to international artist through the crucible of Javanese culture."[8] However, audiences responded favorably, and Gauthier soon included "short talks on Javanese music, batik, and related topics" in her performances.[9] She often wore costumes made from batiked fabrics when she performed, which she claimed were given to her by a queen.[10]

Batik achieved prominence as the American Arts and Crafts movement gained momentum, particularly in New York City's Greenwich Village.[11] In the mid to late 1910s, Wallace established a studio in the Village at 62 Washington Square Park South, where she created batiks. In the Village, Wallace was among other women artists, such as Marguerite Zorach, Martha Ryther, and Amy Mali Hicks, all of whom worked with fiber.[12] These women overcame the pejorative connotation of textile crafts as domestic, and in the context of modernism, the practice of batik presented them with new opportunities for artistic expression.

Wallace's fashions of the 1920s owed a partial debt to "King of Fashion" Paul Poiret, or at least his employment of "the language of Orientalism to develop the romantic and theatrical possibilities of clothing."[13] Yet Poiret was not the first to explore these possibilities; in the mid-nineteenth century, feminists such as Amelia Bloomer experimented "with the appropriation of some aspects of Oriental (Turkish) styling . . . as a dress reform alternative to corsets and hoopskirts."[14] Though Poiret is generally credited as one of the first designers of the modern era to free women from corsets through his embrace of draped silhouettes,[15] his Orientalist aesthetic, which he asserted was authentic, was more accurately "a Russian idea of an Orient as seen by the French," no doubt inspired by the popularity of the Ballets Russes.[16] Poiret perpetuated a visual fantasy that othered cultures of vast geographic regions into fashions for privileged clients in search of the exotic.

The Western fantasy of an Oriental silhouette resulted in the proliferation of voluminous draped garments ideally suited for batik textile designs that appealed to the bohemian set of Greenwich Village and some feminists of the period.[17] *Women's Wear* editor M. D. C. Crawford championed loose-fitting, handmade, ethnographically inspired dress and textiles as part of his strategy to establish a "distinctly American textile and apparel industry."[18] Wallace was an admirer of Poiret's work, and his influence is evident in her designs of the 1920s. When he visited New York City in 1922, she painted his portrait in oil on canvas (Fig. 2). This may have been a study for a batik she intended to create; however, it has been lost to time if it was ever completed.

In 1919, W. G. Bowdoin, a reporter for the *Evening World*, visited Wallace's studio, where he saw many garments made of custom batik fabric, including a Greek negligee and a Chinese boudoir costume, as well as draped garments and other two-piece fancy lounge or "boudoir" ensembles consisting of pants and a jacket.[19] While Wallace was more specific in naming the ethnographic inspiration of her fashions, they were just as contrived in fantasy as Poiret's. Her styles appealed to privileged yet

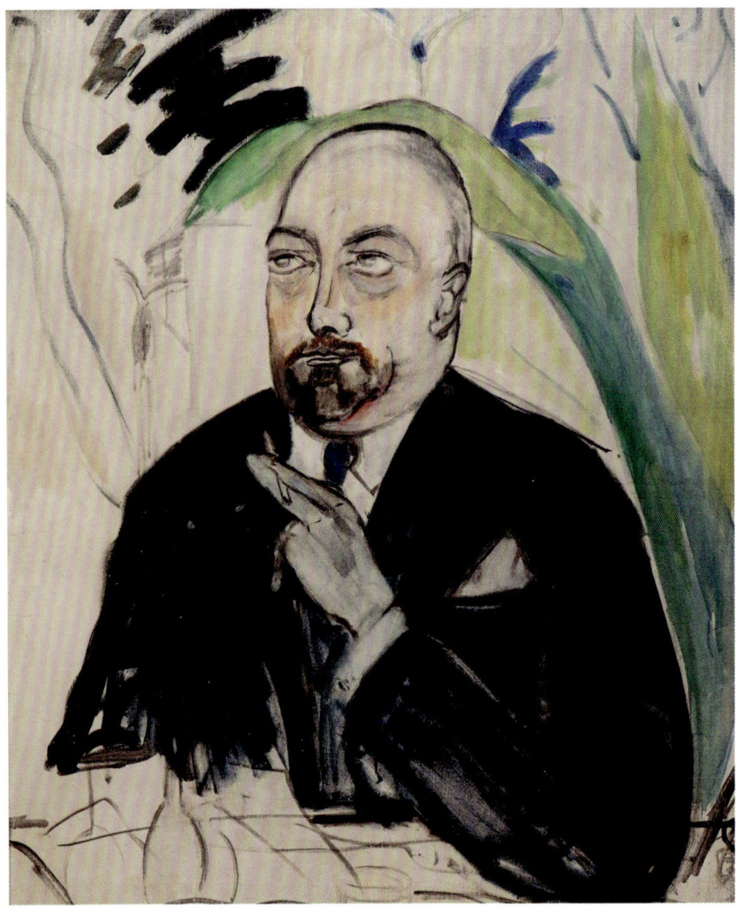

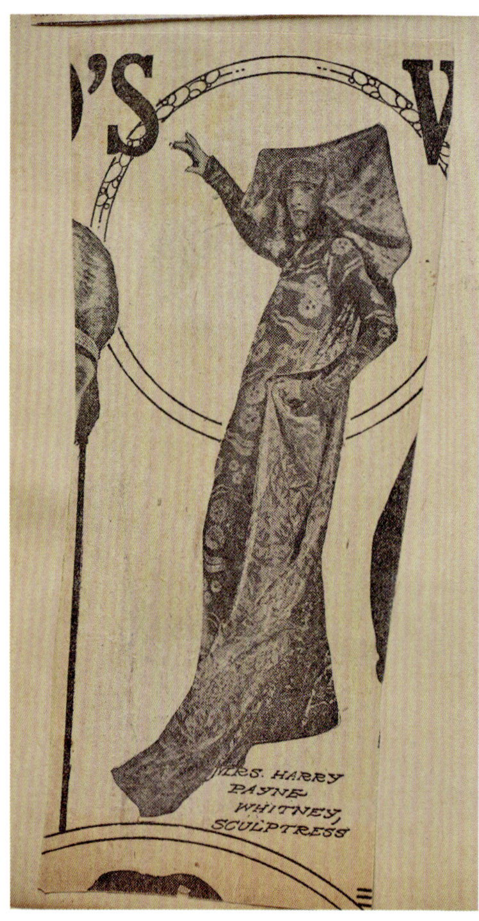

FIG. 2
Ethel Wallace (1886–1968), *Portrait of Paul Poiret*, ca. 1922. Oil on canvas, 42 × 36 inches. Collection of Morrie Breyer and Michael Mamp. (Photo: Adam Sparkes)

FIG. 3
Newspaper clipping showing Gertrude Whitney in a batik gown and headdress by Ethel Wallace, ca. 1922. Ethel Wallace papers. Collection of the late Kristina Barbara Johnson, courtesy of Jeniah Johnson.

FIG. 4
Ethel Wallace in a batik gown of her design, 1919. In "The Fashionable Vogue for Batiks," *Bush Magazine of Factory, Shipping and Sales Economy* (July 1919): 7. Ethel Wallace papers. Collection of the late Kristina Barbara Johnson, courtesy of Jeniah Johnson.

progressive women of the period, such as philanthropist and sculptress Gertrude Whitney. Wallace made at least two fashion ensembles for Whitney. One featured a bold pattern on rich velvet paired with a medieval-inspired headdress (Fig. 3); the other was a tea gown with a "Chinese jacket of silvery satin with a wide batik border of primrose."[20]

An exhibition in 1919 at the Bush Terminal Sales Building in New York City focused solely on batik, featuring work from leading practitioners, including Ethel Wallace and Mary Tannahill, who led a batik group at Columbia University.[21] Bowdoin described the show as "the most elaborate exhibition of batik artwork ever held in the city, if not in this country,"[22] with a particular focus on fashion: "batik work in gowns, blouses, negligees, bags, [and] haberdashery."[23] Gauthier performed Javanese folk songs at the opening and wore a "costume of royal Javanese batik."[24] Wallace designed a voluminous, elegant draped gown of "rich ornamentation and soft lustre" (Fig. 4).[25] The exhibition reflected the Western fascination with all things batik, facilitated by appropriative performance and design practices that perpetuated the colonial othering of the culture and people of Java.

Wallace's fashion designs in batik were often made to order for socialite clients such as Whitney and sold at luxury retailers like Hickson, Bonwit Teller, and B. Altman.[26] She produced a significant amount of yardage for fashion; by 1920, she had made "two thousand yards of crepe de chine and georgette crepe and 500 yards of velvet done in batik for exquisite French embroideries. For evening gowns its softness and individuality make a garment of great distinction. For lingerie batik can scarcely be excelled. The fact that each batik done by original process is a masterpiece and different from any other makes a batik gown a most wonderful item.

Cotton is the material used by the Javanese, who import most of it from England and Holland, although the homespun cotton is occasionally used, and was used for centuries before the coming

water. It is then soaked for several days in cocoanut oil. This in its turn is boiled out in water containing the ashes of burnt rice stalks. The process is continued until the fabric is free from oil.

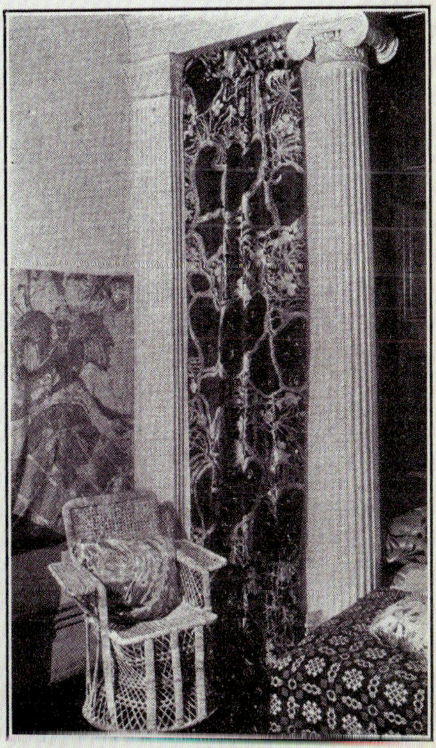

ONE OF THE MOST ADMIRABLE OF THE HOME-CRAFTS. A CORNER DONE IN BATIK.
Photograph courtesy Miss Ethel Wallace.

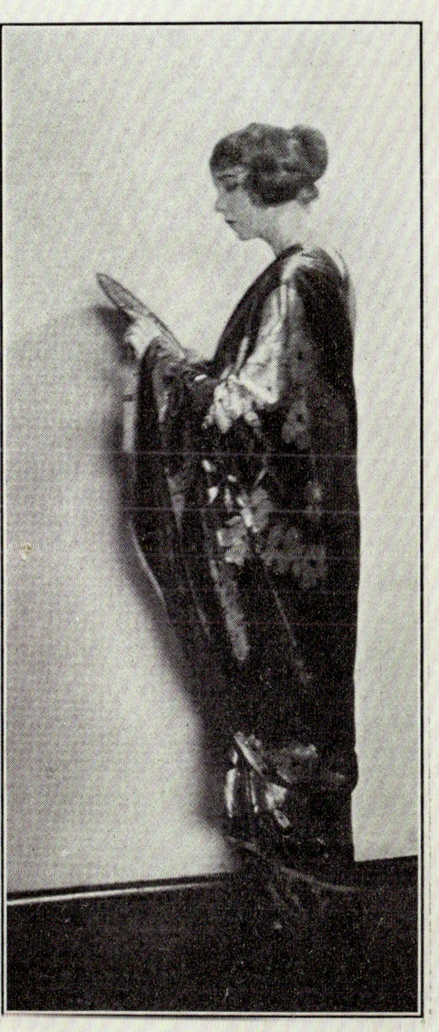

THE RICH ORNAMENTATION AND SOFT LUSTRE OF BATIK LEND DISTINCTION TO ONE'S GOWN.
Photograph courtesy Miss Ethel Wallace.

of the Europeans to Java. The cotton as it comes from the market is not immediately ready to be batiked. If it is a bleached cotton it has to be treated for the removal of the starched chalk and other stiffenings with which it is dressed. This is done by washing it several times in clean cold

The soaking and bleaching are always done whether the material is bleached or unbleached. The process is called "mateng," which, literally translated, means time, or cooked thoroughly.

In Europe and America, however, other methods of producing batik are in vogue. Even ordinary household dyes can be used in garments."[27] One of her batiks, *Chaucer's Garden* (Fig. 5), featured maple leaves, spiderwebs, and white and red lilies.[28] *Chaucer's Garden* was copied and then screen-printed on linen "as an eight-color presentation" by the New York–based purveyor of specialty textiles Robert McBratney & Co.[29] According to a report in *Women's Wear*, Wallace's batik velvets "could be used for picturesque stage costuming, as well as for negligees, evening wraps, and evening gowns."[30] When visiting Wallace's studio in 1920, a reporter for the *Daily Garment News* saw various fashion items, including a "gracefully draped dinner gown, one sleeve of which is lined in rose chiffon . . . [and] an evening cape trimmed with a Patagonia fox collar."[31] An ensemble described in detail was "made of dark green velvet in three pieces, waist, skirt, and over-tunic . . . [It] represents oriental armor, and there is a helmet-like hat to be worn with it . . . a batik design of jade and bronze decorates the dress, monkey fur is used on the sleeves and bodice . . . the hat is a toque effect combined with black velvet and topped with small black ostrich feathers" (Fig. 6).[32] A reporter for the *New York Times* praised Wallace's batiks for fashion as "fine and original work in getting the artist's rather than the craftsman's effect in her designs."[33] Only two batik fashions by Wallace survive to this day; both

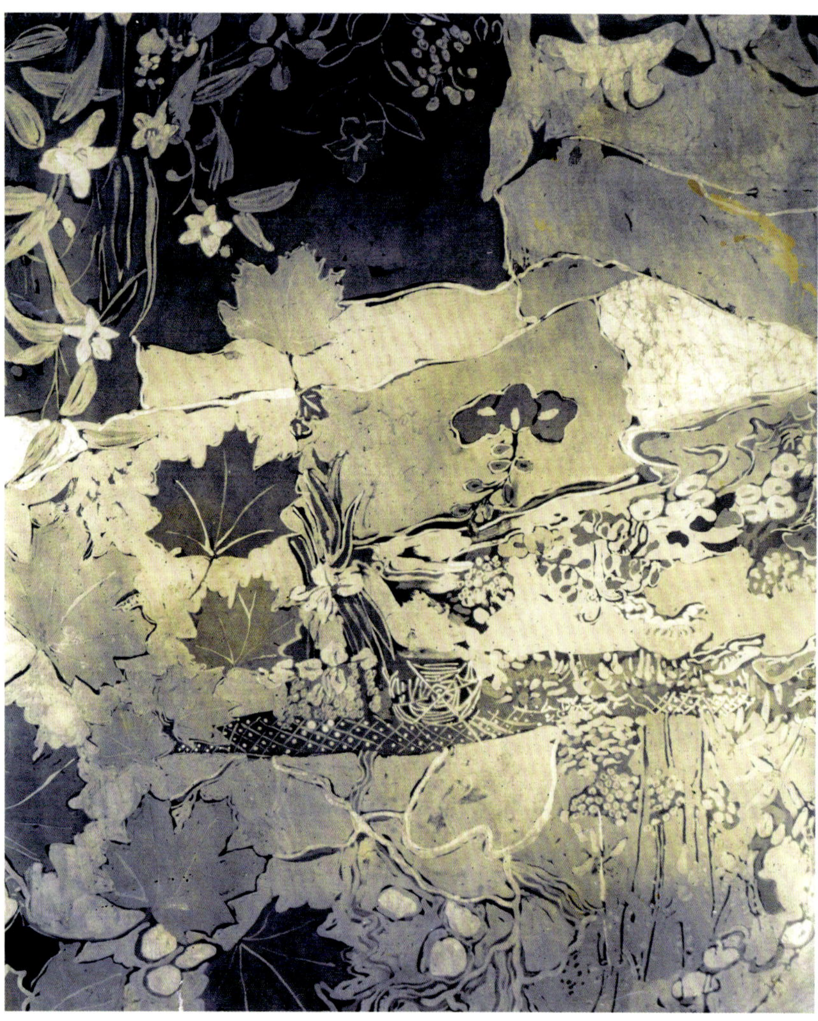

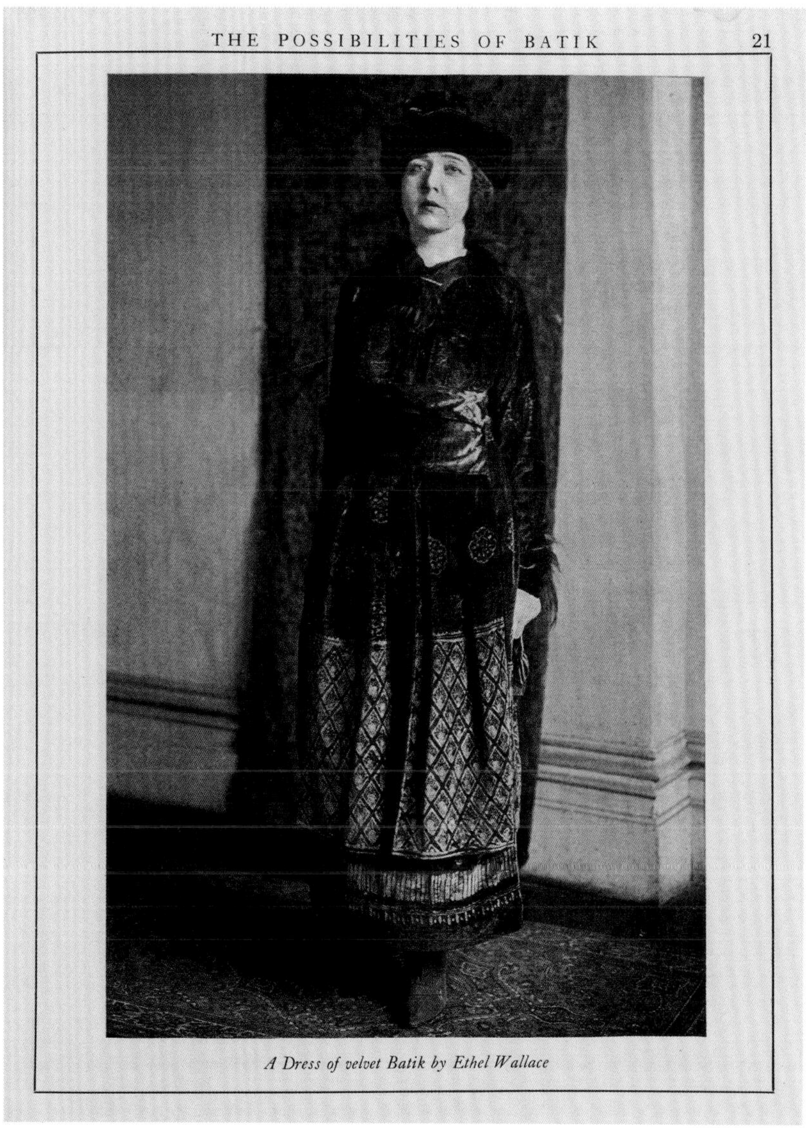

A Dress of velvet Batik by Ethel Wallace

are shown in this exhibition. These examples, each made in a lustrous burnt-orange palette, exemplify the types of fashions Wallace created with her batiks (Figs. 7 and 8). The familiar winding-river motif is abstracted across the surface of the gown, whereas the open-front robe features a delicate floral pattern at the hem and shoulder line.

In June of 1922, Wallace left New York for an extended stay in Paris, where she desired "to interest members of the French couture in her materials."[34] Perhaps her introductions in Paris were facilitated by Poiret. Yet a lack of evidence means her time there remains a mystery. She told colorful stories later in life about her time abroad and her many affairs, especially one with a Spanish count. She spoke less frequently about her relationship with Nathaniel Roberts, whom she wed in 1912. It is probable that while the batik portraits brought her a certain degree of notoriety and respect as an artist, the sale of fabric and fashion produced steady income. Wallace permanently left New York sometime after her husband's death in the early 1930s and once again set up a studio in her father's grist mill in Lambertville, New Jersey.

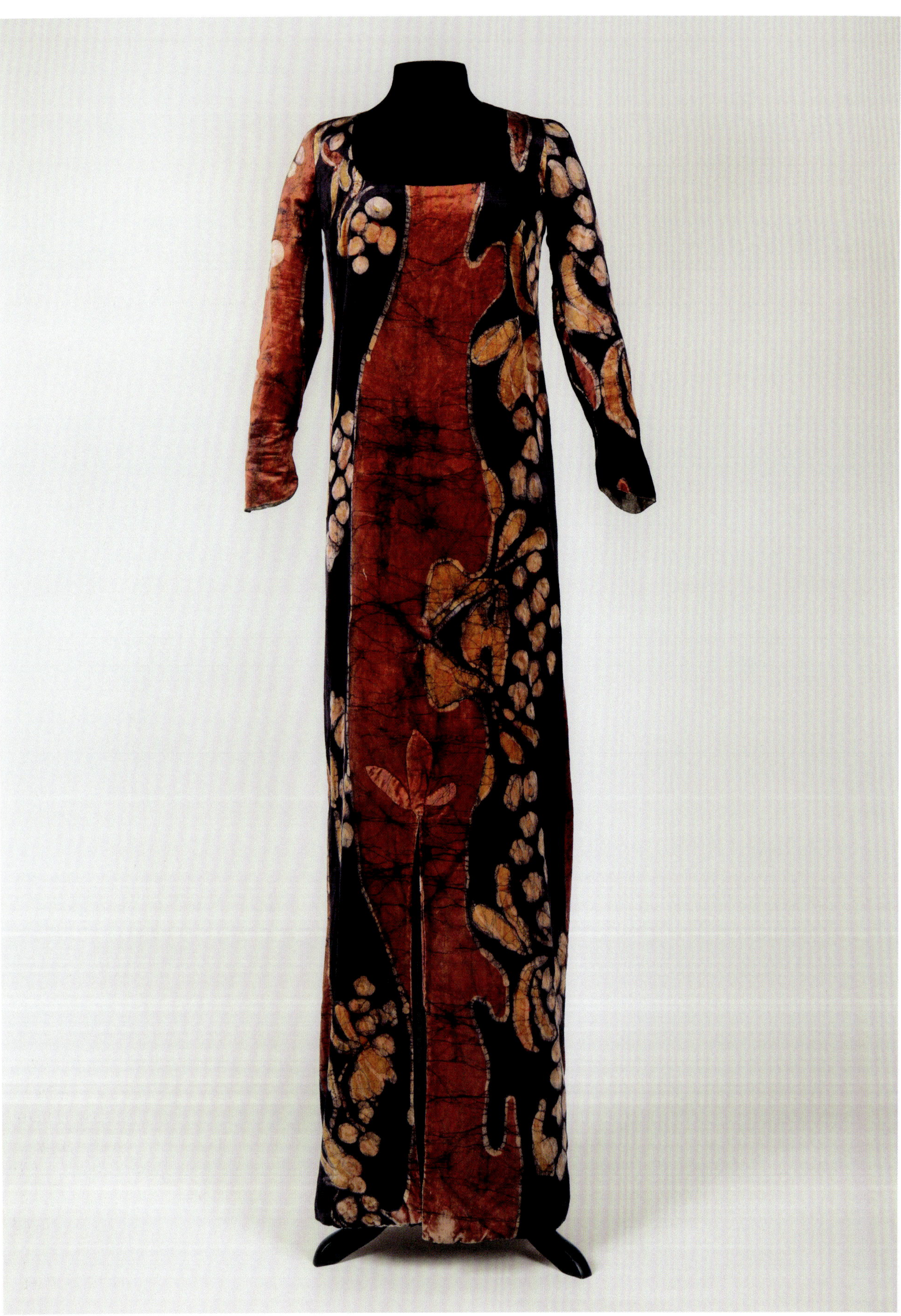

There are few records of Wallace's activity post-1930; however, we know that she initially continued to produce batiks out of a studio in Lambertville. Legend has it that after a series of fires in her studio, she abandoned batik-making, as the chemicals she used were highly flammable and did not mix well with her chain-smoking. In the early 1930s, Wallace bought a house in Bucks County, Pennsylvania, not far from New Hope. She gardened, wrote poetry, painted at least one mural in a private residence, wrote a play for which she designed the sets and costumes, and painted her many cats and flowers from her garden.[35] In 1958, a retrospective exhibition of her work was staged at the Charles-Fourth Gallery in New Hope, Pennsylvania.[36]

Ethel Wallace: Modern Rebel is the first solo exhibition of her work to occur in sixty-five years. Yet her legend has persisted, due in part to colorful stories of her driving around town in an old car with no windshield, dancing the tango at a Phillips' Mill event with a lover who was a man of color, and climbing through a neighbor's window in the middle of the night to leave a jar of lemon butter for their breakfast, to name

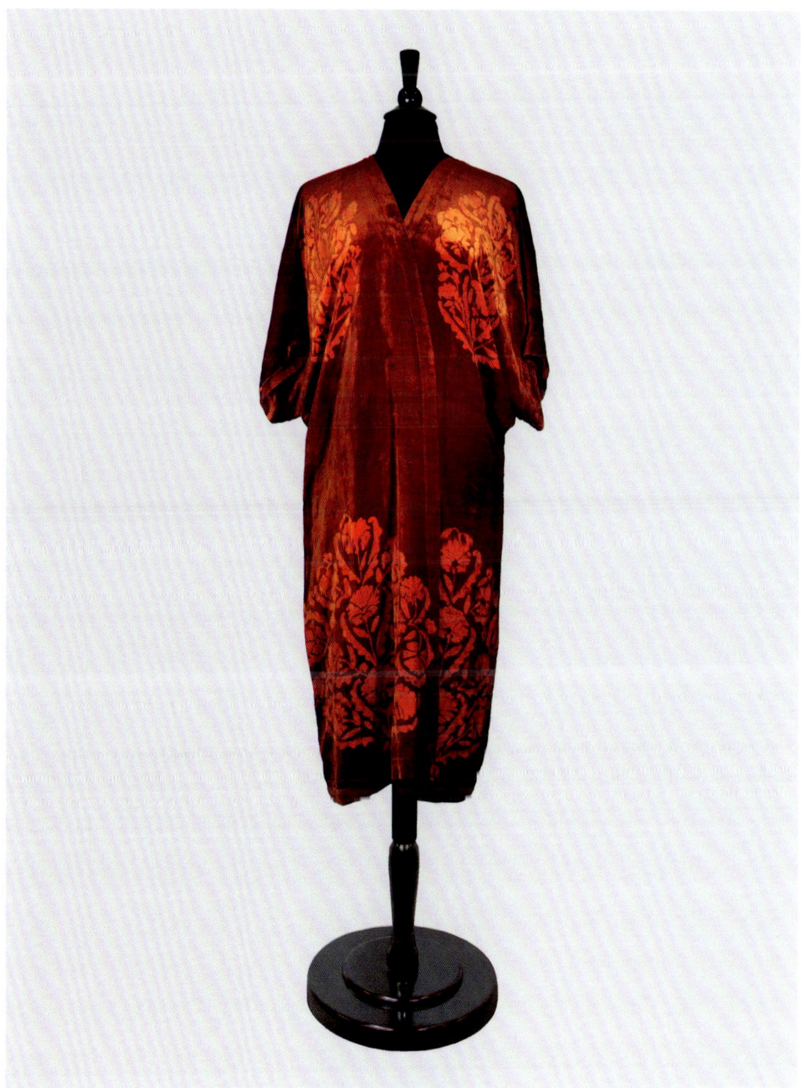

just a few. This is the enduring legacy of an independent woman who was no doubt a rebel in her time. At long last, this exhibition goes beyond the seductive stories to reveal the talents and techniques of an accomplished artist, designer, and craftsperson. Ethel Wallace can now be holistically remembered as a bohemian rebel and a unique and talented woman artist of the early to mid-twentieth century, a long-overdue recognition. Wallace's batiks represent an intersection of modernism and craft and were widely reported upon, well received, and supported by noteworthy individuals. When she passed away in 1968, one obituary described her as "a true Renaissance woman . . . [A] brilliant cook, a fine couturiere, a writer of plays, an artist, an animal lover, a historian, a traveler in her younger days, a raconteur, a woman of endless curiosity, vain about her looks and age, joyous in the face of endless economic adversity, she was indeed something special."[37]

1. Portions of this essay are from my article "Ethel Wallace: A Forgotten History of Batik and Fashion," *Journal of Modern Craft* 14, no. 3 (2021): 253–73, DOI: 10.1080/17496772.2021.2000706.

2. James M. Alterman, *New Hope for American Art: A Comprehensive Showing of Important 20th Century Painting from and Surrounding the New Hope Art Colony* (Lambertville, NJ: Jim's of Lambertville, 2005), 574–77.

3. Frances K. Pohl, *Framing America: A Social History of American Art* (New York: Thames & Hudson, 2008), 309.

4. Maria Wronska-Friend, "Batik of Java: Global Inspiration," in *Textile Society of America Symposium Proceedings* (Vancouver, BC: Textile Society of America, Inc., 2018).

5. Fiona Kerlogue, *Batik: Design, Style and History* (London: Thames & Hudson, 2004).

6. Mary Margaret McBride, "Textile Painting, Art's Newest Idea, Gives Grandad Proper Color Scheme," *Evening Mail*, ca. 1921, Ethel Wallace scrapbook, Ethel Wallace papers, collection of the late Kristina Barbara Johnson.

7. Henry Spiller, *Javaphilia: American Love Affairs with Javanese Music and Dance* (Honolulu: University of Hawaii Press, 2015).

8. Matthew Isaac Cohen, *Performing Otherness: Java and Bali on International Stages, 1905–19* (New York: Palgrave Macmillan, 2010), 50.

9. Matthew Isaac Cohen, "Eva Gauthier, Java to Jazz," *Journal of the Humanities and Social Sciences of Southeast Asia* 164, no. 1 (2008): 47.

10. See Gauthier's archive at the Library and Archives Canada, which includes images of her in batik/Javanese costume.

11. Abby G. Lillethun, "Batik in America: Javanese to Javanesque, 1893 to 1937" (PhD diss., Ohio State University, 2002), 1.

12. Ann Marguerite Tartsinis, *An American Style: Global Sources for New York Fashion and Textile Design, 1915–1928* (New York: Bard Graduate Center, 2013).

13. Harold Koda and Andrew Bolton, eds., *Poiret* (New Haven and London: Yale University Press, 2007), 13.

14. Susan B. Kaiser, *Fashion and Cultural Studies* (London: Berg, 2012), 95.

15. Peter Wollen, *Raiding the Icebox: Reflections on Twentieth-Century Culture* (Bloomington: Indiana University Press, 1993).

16. Nancy J. Troy, *Couture Cultures: A Study in Modern Art and Fashion* (Cambridge, MA: MIT Press, 2003), 104.

17. For an overview of the role of Orientalism in the sartorial choices of some feminists of the early twentieth century, see Einav Rabinovitch-Fox, "[Re]Fashioning the New Woman: Women's Dress, the Oriental Style, and the Construction of American Feminist Imagery in the 1910s," *Journal of Women's History* 27, no. 2 (2015): 14–36.

18. Deborah Saville, "Freud, Flappers, and Bohemians: The Influence of Modern Psychological Thought and Social Ideology on Dress, 1910–1923," *Dress: The Journal of the Costume Society of America* 30, no. 1 (2003): 67.

19. W. G. Bowdoin, "Ethel Wallace: Maker of Batiks in the Village," *Evening World*, July 9, 1919, Ethel Wallace scrapbook, Ethel Wallace papers.

20. "Woman's World and Its Ways: The Batik Room," *Evening Standard*, July 24, 1920, Ethel Wallace scrapbook, Ethel Wallace papers.

21. "Batik Applied to Modern Dress and Interior Decoration," *American Cloak and Suit Review* (September 1919): 133–34.

22. W. G. Bowdoin, "Batik Exhibition at Bush Terminal Sales Building," *Evening World*, August 8, 1922, Ethel Wallace scrapbook, Ethel Wallace papers.

23. Invitation to the opening of the exhibition at the Bush Terminal Building, Ethel Wallace scrapbook, Ethel Wallace papers.

24. "Notes on Current Art," *New York Times*, July 20, 1919, 33.

25. "The Fashionable Vogue for Batiks," *Bush Magazine of Factory, Shipping and Sales Economy* (July 1919): 7, Ethel Wallace scrapbook, Ethel Wallace papers.

26. For mentions of where to buy Wallace's fashions during this period, see M. D. C. Crawford, "Design Department," *Women's Wear*, August 11, 1920, 6; and "Woman Artist Makes Batik: Miss Ethel Wallace Has Created 2,500 Yards of Fabric," *Daily Garment News*, January 5, 1920, Ethel Wallace scrapbook, Ethel Wallace papers.

27. "Woman Artist Makes Batik."

28. "Woman Artist Makes Batik."

29. "Robert McBratney & Co. Inc. Announces a Most Important Addition of Hand Printed Linens," ca. 1919, advertisement clipping, Ethel Wallace scrapbook, Ethel Wallace papers. McBratney had showrooms in New York, Chicago, and Los Angeles.

30. "American Artist," *Women's Wear*, June 14, 1922, 6–7.

31. "American Artist," 6–7.

32. "American Artist," 6–7.

33. "Notes on Current Art," *New York Times*, August 3, 1919, 35.

34. "American Artist," 6.

35. Wallace's archive includes journals with poetry, sketches for theatrical costumes, and photographs of one large mural she completed in a private residence.

36. See *Paintings and Batiks by Ethel Wallace* (exhibition catalogue) (New Hope, PA: Charles-Fourth Gallery, 1958), Ethel Wallace Artist File, James A. Michener Art Museum Library Collection. The exhibit ran from October 27 through November 15, 1958.

37. Mike Ellis, "So Ungiving Are People . . . Except in the Case of Ethel Wallace," Ethel Wallace Artist File, James A. Michener Art Museum Library Collection.

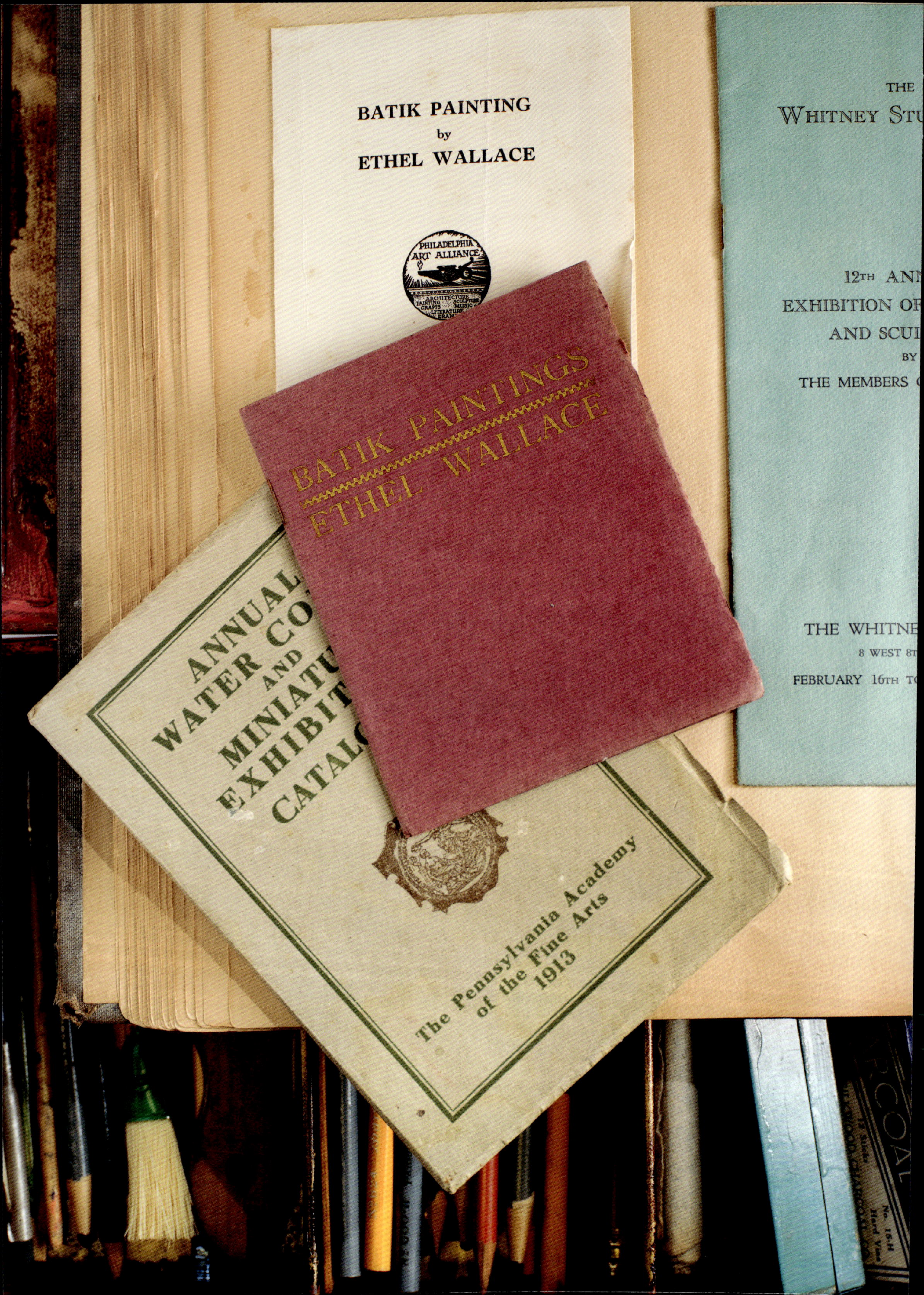
BATIK PAINTING
by
ETHEL WALLACE
PHILADELPHIA ART ALLIANCE
ARCHITECTURE PAINTING SCULPTURE CRAFTS MUSIC LITERATURE DRAMA
BATIK PAINTINGS
ETHEL WALLACE
THE
WHITNEY STU
12TH ANN
EXHIBITION OF
AND SCUL
BY
THE MEMBERS O
THE WHITNE
8 WEST 8T
FEBRUARY 16TH TO
ANNUAL
WATER CO
AND
MINIATU
EXHIBIT
CATALO
The Pennsylvania Academy
of the Fine Arts
1913

Exhibition History

GROUP SHOWS

1910
Annual Exhibition, Pennsylvania Academy of the Fine Arts, Philadelphia

APRIL 17–29, 1913
Exhibition of Paintings, MacDowell Club of New York

NOVEMBER 9–DECEMBER 14, 1913
Eleventh Annual Philadelphia Water Color Exhibition, Pennsylvania Academy of the Fine Arts

SEPTEMBER 27–OCTOBER 17, 1915
Exhibition of Painting and Sculpture by Women Artists for the Benefit of the Woman Suffrage Campaign, Macbeth Gallery, New York

MARCH 1919
Annual Exhibition of the Fellowship of the Pennsylvania Academy of the Fine Arts, Philadelphia Art Alliance

AUGUST 5–15, 1919
Exhibition of Batik Art Work, Bush Terminal Sales Building, New York

SUMMER 1919
Exhibition of Handicrafts and Industrial Arts, Albright Art Gallery, Buffalo, New York; Wallace won the Guild of Allied Arts Prize, in the amount of twenty-five dollars, for her hand-decorated textiles

Second Annual American and European Art Exhibition, Dallas Art Association, Adolphus Hotel, Dallas, Texas

APRIL 1922
Annual Exhibition of Paintings and Sculpture by Members of the Club, Whitney Studio Club, New York

JUNE 1–30, 1922
Exhibition of Modern Painted Screens and Antique Painted Screens, Wanamaker Gallery of Modern Decorative Arts, Belmaison Gallery, New York

FEBRUARY 16–MARCH 5, 1927
Twelfth Annual Exhibition of Paintings and Sculpture by the Members of the Club, Whitney Galleries, New York

JANUARY 1–31, 1928
Exhibition, Columbus Gallery of Fine Arts, Ohio

JULY 1931
Arts and Crafts by Members of the New Hope Art Colony, Van Boskerck Studios, Spring Lake, New Jersey

OCTOBER 10–25, 1931
Forty-Sixth Annual Exhibition of Paintings, Sculpture and Art Objects Assembled and Exhibited by the State Fair of Texas in the Art Department, Dallas

DECEMBER 6, 1931–JANUARY 17, 1932
Exhibition of Local Craft, Reading Public Museum and Art Gallery, Pennsylvania

1934
Exhibition, Independent Gallery, New Hope, Pennsylvania

MAY–JUNE 11, 1936
Allied Arts Exhibition, Phillips' Mill, New Hope, Pennsylvania

SOLO SHOWS

CA. 1919
Solo Exhibition, Philadelphia Art Alliance

JULY 1920
Batik Painting, Leicester Galleries, London

CA. 1921
Ethel Wallace Batik, Galleries of Marie Sterner, New York

APRIL 11–23, 1921
Exhibition of Batik Paintings by Ethel Wallace, Arts Guild Galleries, New York

NOVEMBER 6–21, 1921
Exhibition of Batik Paintings by Ethel Wallace, Neoma Nagel Galleries, Chicago

FEBRUARY 13–25, 1922
Exhibition of Batik Paintings by Ethel Wallace, Studio of Miss Amelia Muir Baldwin, Boston

MARCH 20–APRIL 2, 1922
Ethel Wallace: Textile and Decorative Paintings, Anderson Galleries, New York

FALL 1927
Solo Exhibition, the Blue Mask, New Hope, Pennsylvania

NOVEMBER 23–DECEMBER 7, 1931
Batik Painting by Ethel Wallace, Philadelphia Art Alliance

OCTOBER 27–NOVEMBER 15, 1958
Paintings and Batiks by Ethel Wallace, Charles-Fourth Gallery, New Hope, Pennsylvania

OCTOBER 21, 2023–MARCH 10, 2024
Ethel Wallace: Modern Rebel (retrospective), James A. Michener Art Museum, Doylestown, Pennsylvania

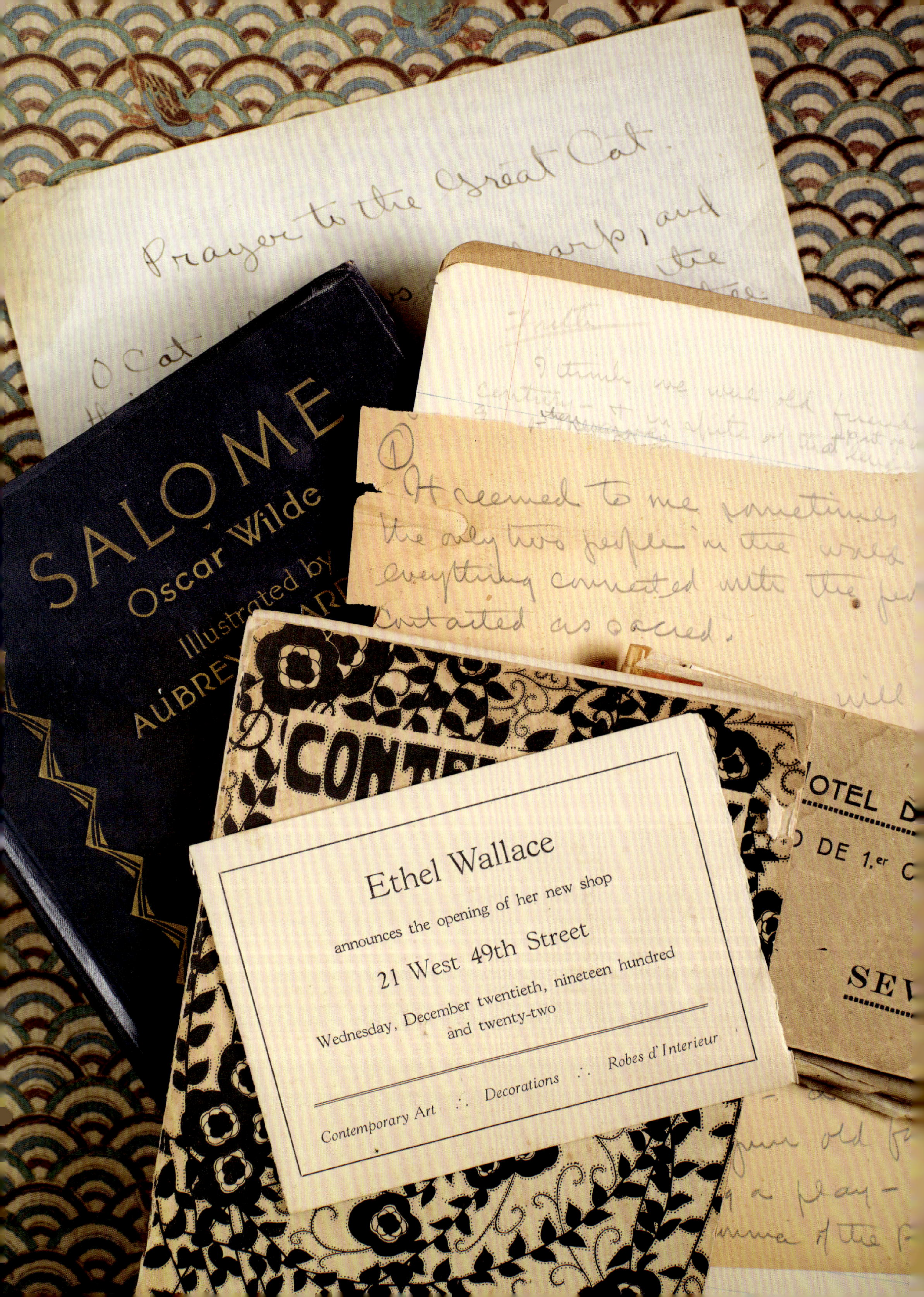
Prayer to the Great Cat.
O Cat—
SALOME
Oscar Wilde
Illustrated by
AUBREY
CONTE
Ethel Wallace
announces the opening of her new shop
21 West 49th Street
Wednesday, December twentieth, nineteen hundred
and twenty-two
Contemporary Art :: Decorations :: Robes d'Interieur
OTEL D
D DE 1.er C
SEV

Acknowledgments

AFTER ALL MY HOURS SITTING AMID STACKS of Ethel Wallace's old things, sifting through a microcosm of a life—the articles and books that she read; the records she kept of her career; the photographs she tucked into decorative cases; the cigarette-burnt, wine-stained pages of her most personal writings—one small set of words, written in her curling handwriting, stays with me: "I think we were old friends—in some century." At many moments throughout my research, I grinned at one of Ethel's quips or marveled at our shared love for cats and all things strange and amusing, and at the end of a day's work I found myself lamenting the stubborn linearity of time. As a woman working exactly one hundred years after Wallace made her way through New York's modernist circles, I've come to admire her persistence and resilience, and time has frequently been on my mind during this project. I've thought deeply about the era in which she lived, fraught with world wars and discrimination yet glimmering, briefly, with the golden aura of the 1920s. And I've wondered what she would think of our current day, in which the hope for a rerun of the Roaring Twenties was dashed by a global pandemic and economic recession, and in which prejudice remains pervasive. There are many things we have in common with Wallace today, and one of them is the people who have bridged the generation between her time and ours to ensure that her work stays alive and receives the celebration it deserves.

Most important among these individuals are the late Kristina Barbara Johnson, Wallace's devoted friend and beneficiary, and Jeniah (Kookie) Johnson, Kristina's daughter, both of whom held on to Wallace's work and belongings all these years and tenaciously advocated for her recognition in Bucks County's artistic history. On behalf of the Michener, I want to thank Jeniah for her patience with this exhibition's long, meandering development. I also want to thank her personally for allowing us to store and access Wallace's archives and textiles at the museum and perform detailed research, without which this exhibition and catalogue would have left far more questions unanswered.

I hope this project inspires further research on Wallace's work, and I am grateful for the research that has already been published by Dr. Michael Mamp, whose essay in this catalogue unveils Wallace's forgotten contribution to fashion and recounts his own unique experience with Wallace and the Johnsons.

We are grateful to the private lenders of this exhibition: Sue Bunkin, Jim Alterman, Darragh Ellerson, Michael Mamp, Jeniah Johnson, and lastly, Edwin Hild, who not only lent to the show but also helped connect me to local community members during my research on Wallace. I want to thank Eleanor Miller for sharing such entrancing memories and stories of Wallace, and Brenda Meredith for taking the time to recount her memories, too.

The Michener's chief curator, Dr. Laura Turner Igoe, has backed this project for years, and her support ensured its fruition. I will always be grateful for her mentorship and feedback, especially in the development of this exhibition and catalogue. In that vein, I also thank Joshua Lessard and Adam Hutler for their work on this exhibition and their willingness to listen and constructively respond to my Ethel-inspired, labyrinthine musings. Barbara Moon Boertzel's research into batik and artists who worked in this medium during Wallace's era was also incredibly helpful in the development of my essay. Ryan Polich and the team at Marquand Books deserve thanks, too, for their gracious assistance in capturing Wallace's character in this beautifully designed catalogue. The catalogue's publication and the conservation of Wallace's work would not have been possible without the financial support of the Richard C. von Hess Foundation, the Coby Foundation, and of Jeniah Johnson and Tom Sheeran. To them we are exceedingly grateful.

Most of all, I am thankful to Ethel Wallace for her exceptional work and ability to reach through time and charm us all, even long after her end.

Tara Kaufman
Associate Curator of Clothing and Textiles
History Colorado

Author Biographies

JENIAH JOHNSON is a writer living in northern Vermont with her artist husband, Tom Sheeran. Born and raised in Princeton, New Jersey, Jeniah (also known as Kookie) began her professional life managing the whaling and folk art collections of her mother, Kristina Barbara Johnson. Jeniah owned and operated two arts-related businesses based in Princeton before taking a career break to spend time with her young children. In 2008, she became director of development and marketing for the Arts Council of Princeton. In 2019, she earned a master of fine arts in writing at the Vermont College of Fine Arts.

TARA KAUFMAN is associate curator of clothing and textiles at History Colorado in Denver. As assistant curator at the James A. Michener Art Museum, she curated *Walé Oyéjidé: Flight of the Dreamer* (2022) and *The Work of Art: Museum Collecting Unpacked* (2022) and co-curated, with Dr. Laura Turner Igoe, *Through the Lens: Modern Photography in the Delaware Valley* (2021). She specializes in modern and contemporary American art, and her research has been supported by the Smithsonian American Art Museum. She received her master of arts in art history from Temple University's Tyler School of Art and Architecture.

MICHAEL MAMP, PhD, is the director and curator of the Textile and Costume Museum at Louisiana State University and an associate professor of fashion and textile history. His research explores American fashion and textile history of the twentieth century. He researched the life and work of Ethel Wallace for over twelve years. Many people made that possible, but none more so than Jeniah Johnson, to whom he is forever grateful.

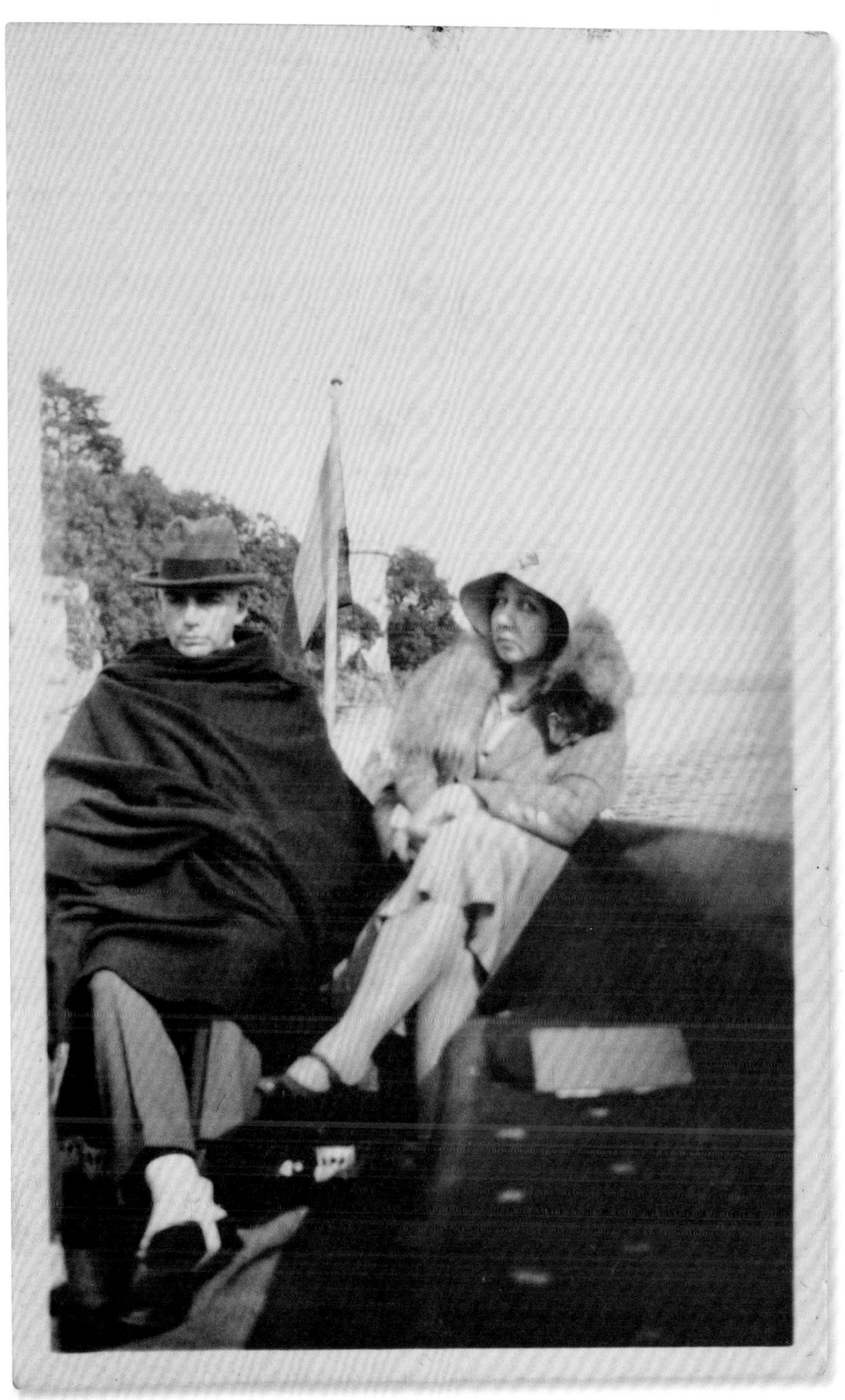

This book is published in conjunction with the exhibition *Ethel Wallace: Modern Rebel*, presented at the James A. Michener Art Museum, Doylestown, Pennsylvania, from October 21, 2023, through March 10, 2024.

The exhibition and catalogue are supported by the Richard C. von Hess Foundation, Jeniah Johnson and Tom Sheeran, the Coby Foundation, Ltd., and the Michener Art Museum's 35th Anniversary Initiative.

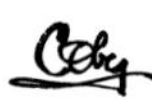 THE COBY FOUNDATION, LTD.

Library of Congress Control Number: 2023935695
ISBN 978-1-879636-15-6

Published by the James A. Michener Art Museum
www.michenerartmuseum.org

Distributed by the University of Pennsylvania Press
www.pennpress.org

Produced by Marquand Books, Seattle
www.marquandbooks.com

Copyedited by Kristin Kearns
Designed by Ryan Polich
Typeset in Bagnard, Bulmer, LTC Globe Gothic, and Walbaum by Brynn Warriner
Proofread by Carrie Wicks
Color management by I/O Color, Seattle
Printed and bound in China by C&C Offset Printing Co.

Page 2: Unknown photographer, *Untitled (Portrait of Ethel Wallace)*, n.d. Photograph, 9⅜ × 6¾ inches. Collection of the late Kristina Barbara Johnson, courtesy of Jeniah Johnson.

Page 4: Sample of a printed fabric by Wallace. Collection of the late Kristina Barbara Johnson, courtesy of Jeniah Johnson.

Page 6: Unknown photographer, *Untitled (Portrait of Ethel Wallace)*, n.d. Photograph, 7 × 4⅞ inches. Collection of the late Kristina Barbara Johnson, courtesy of Jeniah Johnson.

Page 10: Cherry tree at the home of Kristina Barbara Johnson and Jeniah Johnson, ca. 1993. Courtesy of Jeniah Johnson.

Pages 12–13: Sample of a printed fabric by Wallace. Collection of the late Kristina Barbara Johnson, courtesy of Jeniah Johnson.

Page 14: Unknown photographer, *Ethel Wallace Modeling a Batik Garment*, ca. 1920. Photograph, 8¹⁵⁄₁₆ × 5 inches. Collection of the late Kristina Barbara Johnson, courtesy of Jeniah Johnson.

Page 58: Sample of a batik textile by Wallace. Collection of the late Kristina Barbara Johnson, courtesy of Jeniah Johnson.

Pages 70 and 74: Miscellaneous materials from the Ethel Wallace papers. Collection of the late Kristina Barbara Johnson, courtesy of Jeniah Johnson. (Photo: Tara Kaufman)

Page 79: Unknown photographer, *Untitled (Portrait of Ethel Wallace and Unidentified Man)*, n.d. Photograph, 2¹⁵⁄₁₆ × 1¾ inches. Collection of the late Kristina Barbara Johnson, courtesy of Jeniah Johnson.

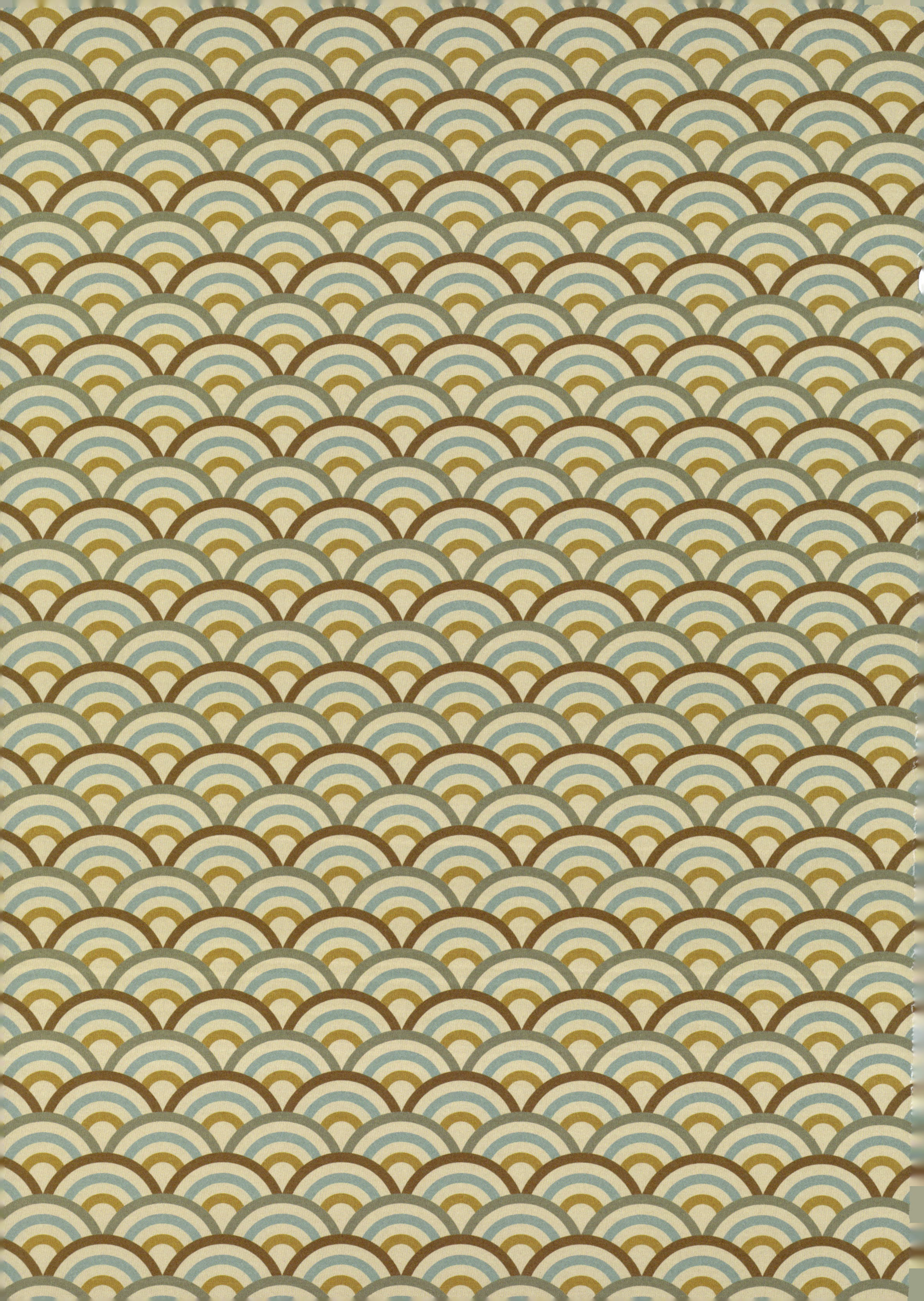